THE KITE RUNNER

Khaled Hosseini

SPARK PUBLISHING

SPARKNOTES is a registered trademark of SparkNotes LLC

Spark Publishing
A Division of Barnes & Noble
120 Fifth Avenue
New York, NY 10011
www.sparknotes.com

ISBN: 978-1-4114-7099-6

Please submit changes or report errors to www.sparknotes.com/errors.

Printed in Canada

10 9 8 7 6 5

CONTENTS

CONTEXT   I

PLOT OVERVIEW   3

CHARACTER LIST   6

ANALYSIS OF MAJOR CHARACTERS   10
    AMIR   10
    HASSAN   11
    BABA   11

THEMES, MOTIFS & SYMBOLS   13
    THE SEARCH FOR REDEMPTION   13
    THE LOVE AND TENSION BETWEEN FATHERS AND SONS   13
    THE INTERSECTION OF POLITICAL EVENTS
        AND PRIVATE LIVES   14
    THE PERSISTENCE OF THE PAST   14
    RAPE   14
    IRONY   15
    REGRESSING IN TIME   15
    THE CLEFT LIP   16
    KITES   16
    THE LAMB   17

SUMMARY & ANALYSIS   18
    CHAPTERS 1–3   18
    CHAPTERS 4–5   22
    CHAPTERS 6–7   25
    CHAPTERS 8–9   28
    CHAPTERS 10–11   31
    CHAPTERS 12–13   34
    CHAPTERS 14–15   37
    CHAPTERS 16–17   40
    CHAPTERS 18–19   43

CHAPTERS 20–21   46
CHAPTERS 22–23   49
CHAPTERS 24–25   52

IMPORTANT QUOTATIONS EXPLAINED   57

KEY FACTS   60

STUDY QUESTIONS & ESSAY TOPICS   62

HOW TO WRITE LITERARY ANALYSIS   65
    THE LITERARY ESSAY: A STEP-BY-STEP GUIDE   65
    A+ STUDENT ESSAY   77
    GLOSSARY OF LITERARY TERMS   79
    A NOTE ON PLAGIARISM   81

REVIEW & RESOURCES   82
    QUIZ   82
    SUGGESTIONS FOR FURTHER READING   88

CONTEXT

KHALED HOSSEINI WAS BORN IN KABUL, AFGHANISTAN, on March 4, 1965, and was the oldest of five children. Just as he describes in *The Kite Runner,* Kabul was a cosmopolitan city at the time. Western culture, including movies and literature, mixed with Afghan traditions, such as kite fighting in the winter. Lavish parties were normal at the Hosseini family's home in the upper middle class neighborhood of Wazir Akbar Khan. Hosseini's father served as a diplomat with the Afghan foreign ministry, and his mother taught Farsi and history at a local high school for girls. Then, in 1970, the foreign ministry sent his father to Iran. While the family only spent a few years there, Hosseini taught a Hazara man, who worked as a cook for the family, how to read and write. By this time, Khaled Hosseini was already reading Persian poetry as well as American novels, and he began writing his own short stories.

Repeated moves marked the next decade of the Hosseini family's life. They returned to Kabul in 1973, the year Mohammad Daoud Khan overthrew his cousin Zahir Shah, the Afghan king, in a coup d'etat. The Afghan foreign ministry relocated the Hosseini family to Paris in 1976. Though they hoped to return to Afghanistan in 1980, that was not possible because of a military invasion by the Soviet Union. Instead, the Hosseinis moved to San Jose, California after they were granted political asylum in the United States. Khaled Hosseini went on to graduate from high school in 1984 and attended Santa Clara University, where he received his bachelor's degree in biology in 1988. In 1993, he earned his medical degree from the University of California, San Diego, School of Medicine, and in 1996 he completed his residency at Cedars-Sinai Medical Center in Los Angeles, making him a full-fledged doctor.

While Khaled Hosseini has said before that his first novel is largely fictional, he acknowledges that the Afghanistan he knew as a child inspired it. Like his main character, Amir, Khaled Hosseini enjoyed Western films and kite fighting. He also lived in a pre-revolutionary Afghanistan that had not yet been ravaged by the Soviet invasion and subsequent Taliban rule. In a 2003 interview with *Newsline,* Khaled Hosseini said the passages in the book most resembling his life are those depicting Amir and Baba as immigrants in the United

States. When the Hosseinis arrived in California, they had difficulty adjusting to the new culture, and for a short time his family lived on welfare. He also remembers the local flea market where he and his father worked briefly among other Afghans, just as Amir and Baba did in the book.

Although the period of adjustment passed and Khaled Hosseini became a successful practicing doctor in 1996, he felt deeply influenced by what he recalled of his homeland, and he began writing *The Kite Runner* in March 2001. Two years later, in the midst of the U.S. war in Afghanistan, Riverhead Books published the book. *The Kite Runner* became an international bestseller, with more than eight million copies in print. It also received numerous book awards, including the the Boeke Prize, the Barnes and Noble Discover Great New Writers Award, and the Literature to Life Award. In 2007, it was made into a feature film. The movie encountered some problems. The children who played Hassan, Amir, and Sohrab, and a fourth boy with a smaller role, had to be moved out of the country. Hassan's rape scene in the film, along with Sohrab's abuse at the hands of the Taliban, put the young actors and their families in possible danger, as some Afghans found the episode insulting. In May 2007, Khaled Hosseini published his second book, *A Thousand Splendid Suns*, which also became a bestseller. In 2013 Hosseini published a third novel, *And the Mountains Echoed*.

Khaled Hosseini's literature also changed his personal life. After nearly twenty-seven years, he returned to Afghanistan to see what had become of his country and his people. Like Amir, he was able to find his father's old home, but he also recognized that war and brutality had destroyed the place where he grew up. His efforts to bring attention to the plight of refugees earned him the Humanitarian Award from the United Nations Refugee Agency in 2006, and he became a U.S. goodwill envoy to the organization. It was during a 2007 trip as an envoy that he was inspired to start his own nonprofit group. He created the Khaled Hosseini Foundation, which funds projects to empower vulnerable groups in Afghanistan, such as women and children. Today, Khaled Hosseini writes full-time. He continues to live in Northern California with his wife, Roya, and their two children.

PLOT OVERVIEW

Amir recalls an event that happened twenty-six years before, when he was still a boy in Afghanistan, and says that that event made him who he is today. Before the event, he lives in a nice home in Kabul, Afghanistan, with Baba, his father. They have two servants, Ali and his son, Hassan, who are Hazaras, an ethnic minority. Baba's close friend, Rahim Khan, is also around often. When Afghanistan's king is overthrown, things begin to change. One day, Amir and Hassan are playing when they run into three boys, Assef, Wali, and Kamal. Assef threatens to beat up Amir for hanging around with a Hazara, but Hassan uses his slingshot to stop Assef.

The story skips to winter, when the kite-fighting tournament occurs. Boys cover their kite strings in glass and battle to see who can sever the string of the opposing kite. When a kite loses, boys chase and retrieve it, called kite running. When Amir wins the tournament, Hassan sets off to run the losing kite. Amir looks for him and finds Hassan trapped at the end of an alley, pinned to the ground with his pants down. Wali and Kamal hold him, and Assef rapes him. Amir runs away, and when Hassan later appears with the kite, Amir pretends he doesn't know what happened. Afterward, Amir and Hassan drift apart. Amir, who is racked with guilt, decides either he or Hassan must leave. He stuffs money and a watch under Hassan's pillow and tells Baba that Hassan stole it. When Baba confronts them, Hassan admits to it, though he didn't do it. Shortly after, Ali and Hassan move away.

The story jumps to March 1981. Baba and Amir are in the back of a truck as they escape from Kabul, which was invaded by the Soviets and has become a war zone. After a hellish journey, they make it to Pakistan. Two years later, Baba and Amir live in Fremont, California. While Baba works at a gas station, Amir finishes high school and goes to college. Baba and Amir sell things at a flea market on Sundays, and Baba sees an old friend, General Taheri. Amir notices General Taheri's daughter, Soraya. When Amir finally speaks to her, General Taheri catches him and tells him there is a proper way to do things. Not long after, Baba is diagnosed with lung cancer. Amir asks Baba if he will get General Taheri's consent for Amir to marry Soraya. General Taheri accepts the proposal. They hold the wedding quickly because of Baba's health, and Baba dies a month later. Amir and Soraya try unsuccessfully to have a baby while Amir works on his writing career.

Amir gets a call from Rahim Khan. Rahim Khan is sick and wants Amir to visit him in Pakistan. Amir meets him a week later, and Rahim Khan tells Amir about the devastation in Kabul. He says things only got worse after the Soviets were forced out. Now the Taliban rule by violence. He has a favor to ask of Amir, but first he needs to tell him about Hassan. When Baba and Amir left Afghanistan, Rahim Khan watched their house. Out of loneliness and because he was getting older, he decided to find Hassan. He convinced Hassan and Hassan's wife, Farzana, to come back to Kabul with him. Farzana and Hassan eventually had a little boy, Sohrab. A few years later Rahim Khan went to Pakistan for medical treatment, but he received a call from a neighbor in Kabul. The Taliban went to Baba's house and shot Hassan and Farzana and sent Sohrab to an orphanage.

Rahim Khan wants Amir to go to Kabul and bring Sohrab back to Pakistan, where a couple lives that will take care of him. He tells Amir that Baba was Hassan's father, and Amir agrees to do it. In Afghanistan, Amir finds the orphanage where Sohrab is supposed to be, but he is not there. The orphanage director says a Taliban official took Sohrab a month earlier. If Amir wants to find the official, he will be at the soccer stadium during the game the next day. Amir goes to the game, and at halftime, the Taliban put a man and a woman in holes in the ground and the official Amir is looking for stones them to death. Through one of the Taliban guards, Amir sets up a meeting with the official.

When they meet, Amir tells the official he is looking for a boy, Sohrab, and the official tells the guards to bring the boy in. Sohrab is wearing a blue silk outfit and mascara, making him appear more feminine and suggesting that the men sexually abuse him. The official says something Amir recognizes, and suddenly Amir realizes the official is Assef. Assef says he wants to settle some unfinished business. He beats Amir with brass knuckles, breaking Amir's ribs and splitting his lip. Sohrab threatens Assef with his slingshot, and when Assef lunges at him, Sohrab shoots him in the eye, allowing Amir and Sohrab to escape. As Amir recovers in the hospital, he finds out there never was a couple to care for Sohrab. Amir asks Sohrab to live with him in the U.S., and Sohrab accepts.

The adoption officials tell Amir that adopting Sohrab will be impossible since he can't prove Sohrab's parents are dead, and

Amir tells Sohrab he may have to go back to an orphanage. Amir and Soraya figure out a way to get Sohrab to the U.S., but before they can tell Sohrab, Sohrab tries to kill himself. He lives, but he stops speaking entirely. Even after they bring Sohrab to California, Sohrab remains withdrawn. One day, they go to a park with other Afghans. People are flying kites. Amir buys one and gets Sohrab to fly it with him. They spot another kite and battle it. Using one of Hassan's favorite tricks, they win. Sohrab smiles, and as the losing kite flies loose, Amir sets off to run it for Sohrab.

Character List

Amir   The narrator and the protagonist of the story. Amir
is the sensitive and intelligent son of a well-to-do
businessman in Kabul, and he grows up with a sense
of entitlement. His best friend is Hassan, and he goes
back and forth between acting as a loyal friend and
attacking Hassan out of jealousy whenever Hassan
receives Amir's father's affection. Amir is a gifted
storyteller and grows from aspiring writer to published
novelist. His great desire to please his father is the
primary motivation for his behavior early in the novel,
and it is the main reason he allows Hassan to be raped.
From that point forward, he is driven by his feelings
of guilt as he searches to find a way to redeem himself.
Ultimately he does so through courage and self-
sacrifice, and he tells his story as a form of penance.

Hassan   Amir's best friend and half brother as well as a servant
of Baba's. Hassan proves himself a loyal friend to
Amir, repeatedly defending Amir when he is attacked
and always ready to listen. His defining traits are
bravery, selflessness, and intelligence, though his
smarts are more instinctual than bookish, largely
because he is uneducated. As a poor ethnic Hazara,
he is considered an inferior in Afghan society, and
he is the victim of racism throughout the novel as a
result. He is Baba's illegitimate child, though he is not
aware of this fact, and he grows up with Ali acting as
his father. His rape is an early catalyst in the story, and
even though he is not present in a significant portion
of the novel, he plays a major role throughout.

Baba   Father of Amir and Hassan and a wealthy, well-
respected businessman. Baba believes first and
foremost in doing what is right and thinking for
himself, and he tries to impart these qualities to
Amir. He also never lets anyone's lack of belief in him
stop him from accomplishing his goals. Although he

distrusts religious fundamentalism, he follows his own moral code and acts with self-assurance and bravery. When necessary, he is even willing to risk his life for what he believes in. Yet his shame at having a child with a Hazara woman leads him to hide the fact that Hassan is his son. Because he cannot love Hassan openly, he is somewhat distant toward Amir and is often hard on him, though he undoubtedly loves him.

Ali   Acting father to Hassan and a servant of Baba's. Ali is defined by his modesty more than anything, and he works diligently as Baba's servant. He loves Hassan deeply, though he rarely expresses his emotions outwardly. Poor and an ethnic Hazara, he suffers from partial paralysis of his face and walks with a limp caused by polio.

Sohrab   Son of Hassan and Farzana. In many ways, Sohrab acts as a substitute for Hassan in the novel, and he is a central focus of the plot in the later sections of the book. He is also an ethnic Hazara and is great with a slingshot. His character arc takes him from being a normal little boy to the traumatized victim of sexual and physical abuse, and he goes from speaking very little to not at all.

Assef   Hassan's and Sohrab's rapist and the novel's antagonist. Assef represents all things wrong in Afghanistan. A racist who wishes to rid Afghanistan of Hazaras, he is incapable of remorse and enjoys inflicting violence and sexual abuse on those who are powerless. He even claims Hitler as a role model.

Rahim Khan Friend of Baba and Amir. Rahim Khan is Baba's closest confidant, and the one man who knows all of Baba's secrets. For Amir, he serves as a father figure, often giving Amir the attention he craves and filling the holes left by Baba's emotional distance.

Farid   Amir's driver and friend. A former mujahedin fighter, Farid is at first gruff and unfriendly. But he becomes a valuable and loyal friend to Amir in Amir's search to find and rescue Sohrab. He is missing toes and fingers from a landmine explosion and represents the difficulties that many Afghans faced in the years of warfare that ravaged the country.

Sanaubar   Hassan's mother and Ali's wife for a time. Though Sanaubar is infamously immoral in her youth and abandons Hassan just after he is born, she proves herself a caring grandmother to Sohrab when she reappears later in the novel.

Soraya   Amir's wife. Soraya is steady, intelligent, and always there for Amir when he needs her. She can be strong-willed like her father, General Taheri, and deplores the way women are often treated in Afghan culture.

General Taheri Soraya's father and a friend of Baba. General Taheri is proud to the point of arrogance at times, and he places great value on upholding Afghan traditions. He is in many ways the stereotypical Afghan male, both in his roles as a father and husband.

Jamila   General Taheri's wife and Soraya's mother. Jamila plays the part of the typical Afghan wife and mother. She obeys her husband without question and wants nothing more than to see her daughter married.

Kamal   A boy from Amir's and Hassan's neighborhood. Cowardly and conformist, Kamal helps Assef rape Hassan. After he is raped himself, he becomes a symbol of the brutality that is destroying Afghanistan.

Sharif   Soraya's uncle. When Sharif first appears, he is just a minor figure at Soraya and Amir's wedding. Later, however, he becomes instrumental in helping to get Sohrab into the United States.

Sofia Akrami Amir's mother. Though Sofia died during childbirth, Amir knows she loved literature, as he does. Amir seeks information about her at various points in the novel.

Farzana Hassan's wife and Sohrab's mother. Farzana appears only briefly, but in that time she is portrayed as a loving mother.

Wali One of the boys from the neighborhood who helps Assef to rape Hassan. Wali is depicted as a conformist.

ANALYSIS OF MAJOR CHARACTERS

AMIR

The central character of the story as well as its narrator, Amir has a privileged upbringing. His father, Baba, is rich by Afghan standards, and as a result, Amir grows up accustomed to having what he wants. The only thing he feels deprived of is a deep emotional connection with Baba, which he blames on himself. He thinks Baba wishes Amir were more like him, and that Baba holds him responsible for killing his mother, who died during his birth. Amir, consequently, behaves jealously toward anyone receiving Baba's affection. His relationship with Hassan only exacerbates this. Though Hassan is Amir's best friend, Amir feels that Hassan, a Hazara servant, is beneath him. When Hassan receives Baba's attention, Amir tries to assert himself by passive-aggressively attacking Hassan. He mocks Hassan's ignorance, for instance, or plays tricks on him. At the same time, Amir never learns to assert himself against anyone else because Hassan always defends him. All of these factors play into his cowardice in sacrificing Hassan, his only competition for Baba's love, in order to get the blue kite, which he thinks will bring him Baba's approval.

The change we see in Amir's character in the novel centers on his growth from a selfish child to a selfless adult. After allowing Hassan to be raped, Amir is not any happier. On the contrary, his guilt is relentless, and he recognizes his selfishness cost him his happiness rather than increasing it. Once Amir has married and established a career, only two things prevent his complete happiness: his guilt and his inability to have a child with Soraya. Sohrab, who acts as a substitute for Hassan to Amir, actually becomes a solution to both problems. Amir describes Sohrab as looking like a sacrificial lamb during his confrontation with Assef, but it is actually himself that Amir courageously sacrifices. In doing this, as Hassan once did for him, Amir redeems himself, which is why he feels relief even as Assef beats him. Amir also comes to see Sohrab as a substitute for the child he and Soraya cannot have, and as a self-sacrificing father figure to Sohrab, Amir assumes the roles of Baba and Hassan.

HASSAN

If Amir's character arc is about growth, Hassan's arc is about not changing at all. From the start and through his death, Hassan remains the same: loyal, forgiving, and good-natured. As a servant to Baba and Amir, Hassan grows up with a very particular role in life. While Amir prepares for school in the morning, Hassan readies Amir's books and his breakfast. While Amir is at school getting an education, Hassan helps Ali with the chores and grocery shopping. As a result, Hassan learns that it is his duty to sacrifice himself for others. Furthermore, by nature he is not prone to envy and he even tells Amir he is happy with what he has, though he sees all the time how much more Amir has. Hassan comes across as the personification of innocence as a result, and this innocence is crucial in creating the drama and symbolism of his rape by Assef. First, Hassan's innocence gives Amir no justifiable reason to betray Hassan. Amir's behavior cannot be rationalized, making it consummately selfish and reprehensible. Second, Hassan's rape becomes the sacrifice of an innocent, a recurring motif in Islam, Christianity, and Judaism that carries a great deal of symbolic meaning.

BABA

In his words and actions, Baba sets the moral bar in the novel. When Amir is a boy, Baba's major concern about him is that he doesn't have the courage to stand up for himself, demonstrating that Baba places great value on doing what is right. If Amir cannot stand up for himself as a boy, Babs worries, he will not have the strength to behave morally as an adult. Baba follows through on these beliefs in his own behavior. When he and Amir flee Kabul, he is willing to sacrifice his life to keep the Russian guard from raping the woman with them, and in doing so he sets the example that Amir will follow later when he must choose between saving himself or doing what he knows to be right.

What the reader sees of Baba from Amir's narrative is not the full story, however. As Amir describes him, he is proud, independent, determined, but sometimes emotionally distant and impatient. We learn from a note Rahim Khan writes to Amir toward the end of

the book that Baba was a man torn between two halves, specifically between Amir and Hassan. Amir never sees Baba's inner conflict because Baba has very much separated his outward appearance
from his internal emotions. For instance, Baba builds an orphanage,
which appears to be a simple act of charity. But as Rahim Khan
explains, Baba built the orphanage to make up for the guilt he felt for
not being able to acknowledge Hassan as his son. Baba's hesitation
to reveal his emotions causes Amir to feel that he never knows Baba
completely, alienating Amir from Baba while Amir is growing up.

The move to America is very difficult for Baba, who is used to
being wealthy and well-respected in his community. He goes from
having wealth and a position of power to working a low-paying job
at a gas station and living modestly. Yet his relationship with Amir
improves. Baba, as Rahim Khan explains in his note, felt guilty over
his rich, privileged life because Hassan was not able to share in it.
When he no longer has his wealth, his guilt diminishes, and with
Hassan not around, he is not straining uncomfortably to act one
way with Amir and another with Hassan. As a result, he is able to
open up more with Amir, and the two grow much closer in Baba's
final years. Despite the fact that he lost everything he had as a refugee, he dies genuinely happy, feeling proud of Amir and perhaps
happy that he was able to build the relationship he always wanted
with at least one of his sons.

THEMES, MOTIFS & SYMBOLS

THEMES

THE SEARCH FOR REDEMPTION

Amir's quest to redeem himself makes up the heart of the novel. Early on, Amir strives to redeem himself in Baba's eyes, primarily because his mother died giving birth to him, and he feels responsible. To redeem himself to Baba, Amir thinks he must win the kite tournament and bring Baba the losing kite, both of which are inciting incidents that set the rest of the novel in motion. The more substantial part of Amir's search for redemption, however, stems from his guilt regarding Hassan. That guilt drives the climactic events of the story, including Amir's journey to Kabul to find Sohrab and his confrontation with Assef. The moral standard Amir must meet to earn his redemption is set early in the book, when Baba says that a boy who doesn't stand up for himself becomes a man who can't stand up to anything. As a boy, Amir fails to stand up for himself. As an adult, he can only redeem himself by proving he has the courage to stand up for what is right.

THE LOVE AND TENSION BETWEEN FATHERS AND SONS

Amir has a very complex relationship with Baba, and as much as Amir loves Baba, he rarely feels Baba fully loves him back. Amir's desire to win Baba's love consequently motivates him not to stop Hassan's rape. Baba has his own difficulty connecting with Amir. He feels guilty treating Amir well when he can't acknowledge Hassan as his son. As a result, he is hard on Amir, and he can only show his love for Hassan indirectly, by bringing Hassan along when he takes Amir out, for instance, or paying for Hassan's lip surgery. In contrast with this, the most loving relationship between father and son we see is that of Hassan and Sohrab. Hassan, however, is killed, and toward the end of the novel we watch Amir trying to become a substitute father to Sohrab. Their relationship experiences its own strains as Sohrab, who is recovering from the loss of his parents and the abuse he suffered, has trouble opening up to Amir.

13

THE INTERSECTION OF POLITICAL EVENTS AND
   PRIVATE LIVES

The major events of the novel, while framed in the context of Amir's life, follow Afghanistan's transitions as well. In Amir's recollections of his childhood, we see the calm state of Kabul during the monarchy and the founding of the republic, and then watch as the Soviet invasion and infighting between rival Afghan groups ruin the country. These events have a hand in dictating the novel's plot and have significant effects on the lives of the characters involved. The establishment of the republic gives Assef an opportunity to harass Amir, simply because Assef's father knows the new president. Later, Kabul's destruction forces Baba and Amir to flee to California. When the Taliban take over after that, they murder Hassan and even give Assef a position that lets him indulge his sadism and sexual urges without repercussions. Both of these events factor into Amir's mission to save Sohrab and his redemption by confronting Assef, subtly implying that Afghanistan will similarly have its own redemption one day.

THE PERSISTENCE OF THE PAST

All the characters in the novel feel the influence of the past, but none so much as Amir and Sohrab. In Sohrab's case, his past has been so traumatizing that it affects all his behavior. The prolonged physical and sexual abuse he endured make him flinch anytime Amir touches him. He also still suffers so much from the abandonment he experienced when his parents died that he attempts suicide when Amir says he may have to go back to an orphanage. For Amir, the past is always with him, from the book's first sentence, when he says he became what he is today at the age of twelve, to its final sentence. That's because Amir defines himself by his past. His feelings of guilt for his past actions continue to motivate him. Amir even feels responsible for the Taliban murdering Hassan, because he thinks he set in motion the events that led to Hassan's death when he pushed Hassan and Ali out of Baba's house. As he says on the book's first page, the past can never be buried.

MOTIFS

RAPE

Rape recurs throughout the novel. The most significant instances of rape are Assef's rape of Hassan and his later rape of Sohrab. Hassan's rape is the source of Amir's guilt, which motivates his search for redemption, while stopping Sohrab's rape becomes Amir's way of redeeming himself. In each case, rape is a critical element in the novel's plot. Other instances of rape include Baba stopping the rape of the woman in the truck with them as they flee Kabul, and the rape of Kamal that Kamal's father implies. As a motif, rape is important for multiple reasons. It is not just physically violent, but it is also an attack on the victim's emotions and dignity. Rape in this sense represents complete physical and mental domination of those who don't have power by those who do, and the victims of rape that we see in the novel, most notably Hassan and Sohrab, always suffer lasting emotional trauma.

IRONY

The adult Amir clearly recognizes the ironies in his own story. He even describes how Rahim Khan tells him when Amir is still a child that he has grasped irony in his writing. The novel's greatest irony, and its most tragic, centers on Amir's choice not to stop Hassan's rape. Amir doesn't intervene because he wants Baba's approval, which he knows he can earn by bringing home the kite and proving that he, like Baba, is a winner. But by not stopping Assef and the others, Amir becomes exactly the sort of coward Baba worried Amir would become, and unwittingly allows Baba's son—and his own brother—to be raped, as he does not yet know that Baba is Hassan's father. Amir ultimately wants to be happy, but instead he earns himself an overwhelming sense of guilt. There is a further irony in the fact that Amir only realizes how much he resembles Baba when he discovers that Baba conceived Hassan with Sanaubar, Ali's wife. Amir wants to share the best of Baba's traits, but instead what they share is the betrayal of their best friends. Another significant irony is the fact that Assef, who raped Hassan and caused Amir's guilt, becomes the way for Amir to atone. Amir is emotionally healed by taking the beating Assef gives him. In each instance, the irony stems from Amir recognizing the unintended consequences of his actions or desires.

REGRESSING IN TIME

Amir does not exactly have flashbacks, which would suddenly put him back in the midst of an earlier event. Instead he repeatedly moves the story back in time to give a history of what he is talking about. The novel begins with him living in San Francisco, for instance, then immediately jumps back to his childhood in Kabul. Shortly after that, he jumps back yet again, this time to Baba and Ali's childhood.

MOTIFS

When he meets Rahim Khan in Pakistan, Rahim Khan starts his own story by going back in time and telling Amir what Hassan's life has been like. Amir tells his story to a reader who has no knowledge of any of this beforehand, and his choice to regress in time and give the backstory of each character does two things: it provides critical information about the character's history, and it also reinforces the thematic idea that the past defines the present.

SYMBOLS

THE CLEFT LIP

Hassan's cleft lip is one of his most representative features as a child, and it is one of the features Amir refers to most in describing him. The split in Hassan's lip acts as a mark of Hassan's status in society. It signifies his poverty, which is one of the things that separates him from Amir, simply because a cleft lip indicates that he and his family do not have the money to fix the deformity. Baba, who is Hassan's biological father, chooses to pay a surgeon to repair Hassan's lip as a birthday gift, signifying his secret fatherly love for Hassan. Later, Assef splits Amir's lip as he beats him, leaving Amir with a permanent scar much like Hassan's. In a sense, Amir's identity becomes merged with Hassan's. He learns to stand up for those he cares about, as Hassan once did for him, and he becomes a father figure to Sohrab. Because of this, it also serves as a sign of Amir's redemption.

KITES

The kite serves as a symbol of Amir's happiness as well as his guilt. Flying kites is what he enjoys most as a child, not least because it is the only way that he connects fully with Baba, who was once a champion kite fighter. But the kite takes on a different significance when Amir allows Hassan to be raped because he wants to bring the blue kite back to Baba. His recollections after that portray the kite as a sign of his betrayal of Hassan. Amir does not fly a kite again until he does so with Sohrab at the end of the novel. Because Amir has already redeemed himself by that point, the kite is no longer a symbol of his guilt. Instead, it acts as a reminder of his childhood, and it also becomes the way that he is finally able to connect with Sohrab, mirroring the kite's role in Amir's relationship with Baba.

THE LAMB

In Islam, as in Christianity, the lamb signifies the sacrifice of an innocent. Amir describes both Hassan and Sohrab as looking like lambs waiting to be slaughtered. Amir says this during Hassan's rape, noting that Hassan resembled the lamb they kill during the Muslim celebration of Eid Al-Adha, which honors Abraham's near sacrifice of his son for God. Similarly, he describes Sohrab as looking like a slaughter sheep when he first sees Sohrab with Assef. Assef and the others had put mascara on Sohrab's eyes, just as Amir says the mullah used to do to the sheep before slitting its throat. Both Hassan and Sohrab are innocents who are figuratively sacrificed by being raped, but these sacrifices have very different meanings. In Hassan's case, Amir sacrifices him for the blue kite. But in Sohrab's case, Amir is the one who stops his sexual abuse. In this context, sacrifice is portrayed as the exploitation of an innocent.

Summary & Analysis

Chapters 1–3

Summary: Chapter 1

The period is December 2001, and our narrator, who tells his story in the first person, recalls an event that occurred in 1975, when he was twelve years old and growing up in Afghanistan. He does not say what happened, but says the event made him who he is. He follows this recollection by telling us about a call he received the previous summer from a friend in Pakistan named Rahim Khan. Rahim Khan asks our narrator, whose name is Amir, to come to Pakistan to see him. When Amir gets off the phone, he takes a walk through San Francisco, where he lives now. He notices kites flying and thinks of his past, including his friend Hassan, a boy with a cleft lip, whom he calls a kite runner.

Summary: Chapter 2

As children, Amir and Hassan would climb trees and use mirrors to reflect sunlight into a neighbor's window, or they would shoot walnuts at the neighbor's dog with a slingshot. These were Amir's ideas, but Hassan never blamed Amir if they were caught. Amir lived with his father, Baba, in a lavish home in Kabul. Meanwhile, Hassan and his father, Ali, lived in a small mud hut on the grounds of Baba's estate, and Ali worked as Baba's servant. Neither Amir nor Hassan had a mother. Amir's died giving birth to him, and Hassan's ran away after having him. One day while the boys are walking, a soldier says to Hassan that he once had sex with Hassan's mother, Sanaubar. Sanaubar and Ali were an unlikely match. Ali was a devout reader of the Koran. The bottom half of his face was paralyzed, and polio destroyed the muscles in his right leg, giving him a severe limp. Sanaubar was nineteen years younger than Ali, beautiful, and reputedly immoral. Most people thought the marriage was arranged by Sanaubar's father as a way to restore honor to his family. Sanaubar openly detested Ali's physical appearance. Five days after Hassan was born, she ran away with a group of traveling performers.

The soldier refers to Hassan as a Hazara, which we learn is a persecuted ethnic group in Afghanistan. The Hazaras originally came from farther east in Asia, and their features were more Asian than Arabic. Hassan's parents were Hazara as well. Amir and Baba, on the other hand, were Pashtun. Once, while looking through history books, Amir discovered information on the Hazaras. They had an uprising during the nineteenth century, but it was brutally suppressed by the Pashtuns. The book mentions some of the derogatory names they are called, including mice-eating and flat-nosed, and says part of the reason for the animosity is because the Hazaras. are Shia Muslim while the Pashtuns are Sunni Muslim.

SUMMARY: CHAPTER 3

Amir mixes his memories of Baba in with this information. Baba was a large man, six feet and five inches tall, with a thick beard and wild, curly hair. According to one story, he even wrestled a bear once. Baba did things people said he could not do. Though he had no training as an architect, he designed and built an orphanage. Though people said he had no business sense, he became one of the most successful businessmen in the city. Though nobody thought he would marry well because he wasn't from a prominent family, he married Amir's mother, Sofia Akrami, a beautiful, intelligent woman who came from a royal bloodline. Baba also has his own strong moral sense. While Baba pours himself a glass of whiskey, Amir tells him that a religious teacher at his school, Mullah Fatiullah Khan, says it is sinful for Muslims to drink alcohol. Baba tells him that there is only one sin: theft. Every other sin is a variation of theft. Murdering a man, for instance, is stealing his life. He calls Mullah Fatiullah Khan and men like him idiots.

Amir tries to please Baba by being more like him but rarely feels he is successful. He also admits to feeling responsible for his mother's death. Since Baba likes soccer, Amir tries to like it as well, albeit unsuccessfully. What Amir is good at is poetry and reading. But he worries his father does not see these as manly pursuits. When he and Baba go to see a match of *buzkashi*, a popular game in Afghanistan in which a rider must put an animal carcass in a scoring circle while other riders try to take it from him, a rider is trampled after falling from his horse. Amir cries, and Baba can barely hide his disdain for the boy. Amir later overhears Baba talking to his business associate, Rahim Khan, the man who later calls Amir from Pakistan. Baba says Amir is not like other boys, and he worries that if Amir can't stand up for himself as a child, he will not be able to do so as an adult.

ANALYSIS

The first three chapters set out the basic facts of the story, including who the major characters are, their backgrounds, and what their relationships with each other are like. The section also establishes a context for the information: Amir, our narrator, is an adult living in the United States and looking back on his childhood years in Afghanistan. In fact, history is an important theme in the novel, and looking back on the past is a recurring motif. That's because, for Amir, the past is not over. He believes it to be a fundamental part of who he is, and no matter how far he is in time or location from his childhood in Afghanistan, the events of that period are always with him. Though it remains unclear why, he feels a tremendous sense of guilt about those events and he believes they shaped him into who he is. This guilt, in fact, informs the entire narrative. Appropriately, he opens the novel in the present then quickly jumps back in time.

The author, Khaled Hosseini, spends much more time on characterization than action in this section. In terms of plot, little happens. Instead, Hosseini introduces us to the personalities of the characters. We learn that Amir is sensitive, bookish, sometimes selfish, and a little mischievous. He is eager to please Baba, whom he views as a role model he can never live up to. Yet he feels Baba does not love him because he is not like Baba and because it was during his birth that his mother died. Baba, meanwhile, is gruff, hardworking, a little distant from Amir, and very much an independent thinker. Anytime someone said he would fail, he didn't listen, and he always succeeded. He doesn't always listen to religious authorities either, evidenced by the fact that he disregarded Mullah Fatiullah Khan, who said it was a sin to drink alcohol. Ali, meanwhile, is dutiful, modest, and quiet. Lastly there's Hassan, who is a loyal and courageous friend. When Amir is threatened, Hassan intervenes. He has his own vulnerabilities, however, particularly regarding his mother.

Significantly, both Hassan and Amir have lost their mothers. They have only their fathers and each other. The relationship between fathers and sons, and between the older generation and the new one, is a major theme of the story. Also, in many ways Amir and Hassan act for each other as a kind of substitute parent, looking out for each other and providing companionship. They are closer than regular friends. They are more like brothers who are on occasion reminded that one is Pashtun and one Hazara. Their relationship plays a central role in the book, and it figures in another theme that is introduced in this section: standing up for what is right. The theme is introduced primarily through Baba, who worries that if Amir can't stand up for himself as a young boy, he may not be able to stand up for what is right as an adult. He says this because he sees Hassan standing up for Amir in fights while Amir appears to back down.

The section additionally introduces the reader to Kabul, the capital of Afghanistan and the location of the events. Khaled Hosseini's main audience for the book is not Afghan, and he familiarizes his readers with life in Afghanistan by explaining some basic facts. Using the characters of Baba and Amir on one side and Ali and Hassan on the other, he lays out all the divisions—economic, ethnic, and religious—present in the country during the late 1970s. Baba and Amir, for instance, are rich and live in a large mansion, while Ali and Hassan are poor and live in a small hut on Baba's property. Related is the difference in the health of the rich and the poor; the poor cannot afford proper medicine. Baba and Amir are both healthy, but Ali and Hassan both suffer from problems affecting their faces. Furthermore, Baba and Amir embody the Pashtun population, whereas Ali and Hassan are part of the Hazara minority, a group subjected to relentless racism in Aghanistan. A related divide in religions is also present: like most Pashtuns, Baba and Amir are Sunni Muslim, while Ali and Hassan, like most Hazaras, are Shia Muslim. (The difference between Sunni and Shia is something like the difference between Catholic and Protestant Christians; Sunni and Shia Muslims share the fundamental beliefs of Islam, that there is only one God and that Muhammad was his prophet for instance, but some of their other beliefs and practices differ.)

An additional divide hinted at in this section is the one between Islamic fundamentalists, such as Amir's teacher, Mullah Fatiullah Khan, and more liberal Afghans like Baba. Baba's words in chapter 3 foreshadow the eventual takeover of Afghanistan by the radical Islamic fundamentalists called the Taliban. "God help us all if Afghanistan ever falls into their hands," he says, after calling Mullah Fatiullah Khan and those like him "self-righteous monkeys" (p. 17). It will be decades before this happens in the novel, but the political events leading up to the rise of the Taliban, beginning in the 1970s and continuing through 2001, will play a major role throughout the book.

CHAPTERS 4–5

SUMMARY: CHAPTER 4

The story jumps back in time to 1933, the year Baba is born and Zahir Shah becomes king of Afghanistan. Around the same time, two young men who are driving while drunk and high hit and kill Ali's parents. Amir's grandfather takes the young Ali in, and Ali and Baba grow up together. Baba, however, never calls Ali his friend. Similarly, because of their ethnic and religious differences, Amir says as a child he never thought of Hassan as a friend. Even so, Amir's youth seems to him like a long stretch of playing games with Hassan. But while Amir would wake up in the morning and go to school, Hassan would clean the house and get groceries. Amir often read to Hassan, who was illiterate. Their favorite story was "Rostam and Sohrab," in which Rostam fatally wounds Sohrab in battle and then finds out Sohrab is his lost son.

During one reading session under their favorite pomegranate tree, Amir begins to make up his own story while he is reading to Hassan. Hassan says it is one of the best stories Amir has read. That night, Amir writes his first short story, about a man whose tears turn to pearls. The man finds new ways to make himself sad so he can cry and become richer, until the story ends with him sitting atop a mound of pearls, sobbing over the wife he has stabbed. Amir tries to show Baba the story while Baba is speaking with Rahim Khan, but Baba does not pay much attention. Rahim Khan takes the story instead. When Rahim Khan leaves later that night, he gives Amir a note. In the note, he tells Amir he has a great talent. Amir goes to where Hassan sleeps and wakes him so he can read him the story. When Amir has finished, Hassan tells him the story is terrific. He has only one question: why didn't the man make himself cry with onions? Amir is annoyed he didn't think of it himself and has a nasty thought about Hassan being a Hazara, though he says nothing.

SUMMARY: CHAPTER 5

One night, gunfire erupts in the street. Ali, Hassan, and Amir hide in the house until morning. Amir says that night was the beginning of the end of the Afghanistan they knew. It slipped away further in 1978 with the Communist takeover, and it disappeared completely in 1979 when Russia invaded. The gunshots were part of a coup in which Daoud Khan, the king's cousin, took over the government. Because the roads are closed that night, Baba doesn't arrive home till dawn. That morning, Amir and Hassan hear talk of what happened on the radio, but they don't understand what it means that Afghanistan has become a republic. They decide to go climb a tree.

While they're walking, a rock hits Hassan. Amir and Hassan discover Assef and two other boys from the neighborhood. Assef is a notorious bully. He is one of the children who mocks Ali's limp and calls him names. He also carries a set of brass knuckles. Assef calls Hassan a flat-nose and asks if they heard about the new republic. He says his father knows Daoud Khan, and that next time Daoud Khan is over for dinner he's going to talk to him about Hitler. Hitler had the right idea about ethnic purity. Afghanistan is the land of Pashtuns and the Hazaras just pollute the country. Assef takes out his brass knuckles. He says Amir is part of the problem for being friends with a Hazara. For a moment, Amir thinks that Hassan is his servant, not his friend, but he quickly recognizes his thought is wrong. As Assef goes to hit Amir, Assef suddenly freezes because Hassan has his slingshot aimed at him, which allows Amir and Hassan to get away.

After Daoud Khan's coup, life goes back to normal. The following winter, on Hassan's birthday, Ali calls Hassan inside. Baba is waiting for him with a man named Dr. Kumar, a plastic surgeon. He is Hassan's present. Dr. Kumar explains that his job is to fix things on people, sometimes people's faces. Hassan touches his lip in recognition. The surgery works, and though Hassan's lip is raw and swollen while he recovers, he smiles all the while. The winter after, all that remains of his cleft lip is a faint scar.

ANALYSIS

The relationship between ordinary people, such as Hassan and Amir, and political events like Daoud Khan's coup are a main focus of this section. At the beginning of this section, for instance, Amir says in his narration that Baba was born in 1933, the same year Zahir Shah became king. Why does Hosseini set up this parallel? Because the fates of Zahir Shah and Baba—as well as the fates of those dependent on Baba, like Amir, Hassan, and Ali—are all bound together in a sense. When Daoud Khan, in a bloodless coup, takes over in chapter 5, we know that the lives of our characters are about to change, even if we aren't sure how. Amir and Hassan's encounter with the racist Assef is a hint: the change is not going to be for the better. The rules that govern life in Kabul have been stirred up, and power balances have shifted. Bloodshed and violence may be in store. We witness this from the perspective of Amir, a young boy who does not know what it means that Afghanistan has become a republic. What he does know is this bully, Assef, suddenly has more power because of who his father knows. Amir feels uncertain and threatened, as many Afghans likely did.

Amir also talks about how prevalent American culture was in the country during this time. The movies Amir and Hassan love most are Westerns starring American actors, notably John Wayne and Charles Bronson. The movies are dubbed into Farsi, and the boys spend their money on Coca-Cola, one of America's biggest exports, as well as Afghan snacks like rosewater ice cream and pistachios. Baba even drives a black Ford Mustang, which Amir points out is the same car that the actor Steve McQueen drives in the American movie "Bullitt." Though Assef, the bully, never speaks of these things specifically, he does talk about Afghanistan's purity. It is not just ethnic purity that Assef and others like him are after, but also cultural purity. The aim is a pure Pashtun people and culture, and the prevalence of American culture in Afghanistan threatens this goal. As a result, the influence of American culture in Afghanistan will be wiped out almost entirely during the years that Amir calls the end of Afghanistan as they know it.

In fact, the overall theme of the section is change, in politics, in society, and in the personal lives of Amir and Hassan. In chapter 4, for instance, Amir recognizes his gift for storytelling, first when he strays from the text he is reading to Hassan and then when he writes his own short story. Simply based on the fact that Amir is narrating the story we are reading, the reader can guess that writing this story is a significant moment in Amir's life, and that Amir will use his talent for a purpose. Hassan also undergoes a change: his cleft lip is repaired. The deformity is something Hassan has known all his life. It is, in a way, a marker of who he is: a poor servant boy. The surgery removes that marker, and again it is as if a balance is upset. We can expect things to change between the boys, though it is unclear at this point how they will change.

The adult Amir, who is telling the story, recognizes several things about his younger self that he evidently didn't realize while he was still a boy. He sees that he was selfish, for example, that he wanted to be the best at everything and didn't want Hassan to be as good. The young Amir genuinely felt that Hassan was beneath him because of Hassan's poverty, ethnicity, religion, and deformity. Whenever Hassan does something that earns Baba's love and respect, Amir lashes out at him in his thoughts. If Hassan is better at something than Amir, like solving riddles, Amir stops doing it. If Amir knows something Hassan doesn't, such as vocabulary words, Amir teases him for his ignorance. In each case, Amir recognizes what he is doing just after the fact and feels guilty. But the reader is led to believe that whatever the event is that changed Amir's life is something he was not able to take back, and so the guilt has haunted him into adulthood.

The reader also sees how the young Amir continues to struggle with his inability to please Baba. This inability makes Amir jealous of anyone else receiving Baba's attention, which is why Amir becomes angry anytime Baba praises Hassan, and again when Baba pays for Hassan's plastic surgery. Amir often finds passive-aggressive ways to take his frustration out on Hassan, such as mocking his ignorance or his inability to read. Reinforcing the theme of the love and tension between fathers and sons that recurs throughout the story is Amir and Hassan's favorite story, "Rostam and Sohrab," which is about a father that fatally stabs an opponent not knowing until too late that the opponent is his son. For Amir, the story represents his relationship with Baba. Complicating Amir's feelings toward Baba further is his relationship with Rahim Khan. Rahim Khan read Amir's story when Baba would not, giving Amir the attention and approval he craved, and Amir even wishes at that point that Rahim Khan were his father. The fact is, Amir desperately wants Baba's approval, yet he has no idea how to get it.

Chapters 6–7

Summary: Chapter 6

For boys in Kabul, winter is the best time of year. The schools close for the icy season, and boys spend this time flying kites. Baba takes Amir and Hassan to buy kites from an old blind man who makes the best in the city. The highlight of the winter is the annual kite-fighting tournament, when boys battle kites by covering the strings in broken glass. When a string is cut, the losing kite flies loose, and boys called kite runners chase the kite across the city until it falls. The last fallen kite of the tournament is a trophy of honor. Hassan is the best kite runner in Kabul, and seems to know exactly where a kite will land before it comes down.

Summary: Chapter 7

In the winter of that year, 1975, the tournament is held in Amir's neighborhood. Usually each neighborhood has its own competition, but the nearby districts will compete together this time. A few days before the tournament, Baba casually tells Amir he may win. An overwhelming desire to win seizes Amir as Amir thinks this will earn him Baba's approval. The day of the competition comes. The tournament lasts all day, and Amir is doing well. He can see Baba sitting on a rooftop, watching. Eventually all that remain are Amir's kite and one other, a blue kite. They battle and Amir wins, sending the blue kite flying loose. Amir and Hassan cheer and hug, but Amir sees Baba motioning for them to separate. Hassan vows to bring the kite back for Amir and sets off.

Amir reels in his kite and accepts everyone's congratulations, then goes looking for Hassan, asking neighbors if they saw him. One old merchant asks Amir what he is doing looking for a Hazara. Amir replies that the Hazara is the son of his father's servant. The old man looks at him distrustfully, but finally tells Amir he saw the Hazara going south. He adds that the boys chasing him have probably caught him by now. Amir searches the neighborhood until he comes to an alleyway. Hassan has the blue kite, and he is surrounded by Assef and the two other boys who are always with him, Kamal and Wali. Amir watches from around the corner. Assef tells Hassan they will let him go only if he hands over the kite. Hassan refuses. He ran the kite fairly, and it belongs to Amir. Assef says Amir would not be as loyal to him, an ugly pet Hazara. Hassan is not shaken. He says he and Amir are friends. Assef and the other boys charge Hassan. Amir almost says something, but ultimately he only watches.

Amir remembers something. He and Hassan fed from the same breast, that of a Hazara woman named Sakina. He recalls going to a fortune-teller with Hassan. They each give the fortune-teller money. The man looks at Hassan. After a moment he puts the money back in Hassan's hand. Then Amir thinks of a dream: he is lost in a snowstorm until a familiar shape appears before him. Suddenly the snow is gone. The sky is blue and filled with kites. Amir looks down the alley where Assef and the others have Hassan pinned to the ground without his pants. Wali says his father believes what they are considering doing to Hassan is sinful, but Assef says he is only a Hazara. The boys refuse, but agree to hold Hassan down. Assef raises Hassan's bare rear end into the air and takes down his own pants. Amir debates doing something, but instead runs away. Fifteen minutes later Amir sees Hassan coming toward him. He pretends he was looking for Hassan, who is crying and bleeding. He hands Amir the kite and neither boy speaks about what happened. When they arrive home, Baba hugs Amir, who presses his face into Baba's chest and weeps.

ANALYSIS

Many of the tensions that have been building till now, such as the treatment of Hazaras by Pashtuns, Amir's desperation to please his father, and the question of whether he can stand up for what is right, come together in the events of this section. The central event is Hassan's rape, and it will be the catalyst that propels the rest of the novel forward. This event is the source of the guilt Amir feels as an adult, and it is why the image of the alleyway, the place where Hassan was raped while he stood by and watched, stays with him. Hassan, we are led to infer, is the kite runner of the book's title, and Amir tells us the story both as a confession and an act of penance. He wants to atone for his sins, and in fact atonement will become a major theme. Two other important themes also converge in the single image of Amir struggling with the decision to intervene or not while Assef, a rich Pashtun boy with a powerful father, rapes Hassan, a poor Hazara. This image conveys the challenge and importance of doing what is right, and the rape of Afghanistan's powerless by those who have power.

In terms of Amir's character growth, his desperation to please his father, which we have witnessed throughout the story, plays a significant part in causing the events of the section. Although Amir feels paralyzed by fear when he sees what is happening, he admits that his main reason for not intervening is selfish. When Baba was a boy, he won the kite-fighting tournament. Though Amir had always done well in the competition, even making it to the final three once, he had never won. To finally please Baba, Amir feels he must show Baba he is like him by winning the tournament and bringing home the kite of his final opponent. Only then will Baba forgive Amir for killing the woman who was Baba's wife and Amir's mother. Amir does not stop Assef from raping Hassan first and foremost because he wants the kite to bring to Baba, and Hassan is the price he has to pay.

Amir describes Hassan, as Hassan is about to be raped, as having a look that he recognizes. It is the way the lamb looks as it is about to be sacrificed for the Muslim holiday Eid Al-Adha, or Eid-e-Qorban, as Afghans call it (in English it is called The Feast of the Sacrifice). The sacrifice of the lamb is meant to celebrate the faith of the prophet Ibrahim, or Abraham as he is called in the West, who was willing to kill his son for God, but who was stopped at the last minute. Islam, Judaism, and Christianity all, in fact, share the symbol of the sacrificial lamb. In Christianity, for instance, Jesus, whom Christians believe died as a sacrifice in order to secure humankind's redemption, is sometimes referred to as the lamb. In this situation, Hassan becomes the lamb and Amir holds the knife.

A terrible irony exists in the fact that Amir allows his friend to be raped in exchange for a prize that he believes will earn him Baba's love. Baba's greatest concern regarding Amir is that he will grow up to be a man who can't stand up for what is right, evident in what he said to Rahim Khan earlier in the novel. If Amir had stood up for Hassan, losing the kite in the process, he would have proved that he had the courage to do the right thing even when it was frightening or dangerous to do so. Perhaps more than by any other action, he would have shown Baba that he was like him. Instead, he ran away because he wanted the kite to please Baba, inadvertently doing exactly the opposite of what Baba would have wanted. As the adult Amir narrates his story, he seems to be aware of the irony of his own history, and he even hints at it earlier in the novel, when he describes Rahim Khan telling him that his understanding of irony is clear from his story about the man who cries pearls.

CHAPTERS 8–9

SUMMARY: CHAPTER 8

After the rape, Amir and Hassan spend less time together. Baba and Amir take a trip to Jalalabad and stay at the house of Baba's cousin. When they arrive they have a large traditional Afghan dinner. Baba proudly tells everyone about the kite tournament, but Amir does not enjoy it. After dinner, they all lie down to bed in the same room, but Amir cannot sleep. He says aloud that he watched Hassan get raped, but nobody is awake to hear him. He says that this is the night he became an insomniac. When Amir and Baba return home, Hassan asks Amir if he wants to walk up the hill with him. They walk in silence, and when Hassan asks if Amir will read to him, Amir changes his mind and wants to go home.

Amir continues not to play with Hassan. When Hassan asks Amir what he did wrong, Amir tells Hassan to stop harassing him. After that, the boys avoid each other. One day, Amir asks Baba if he would ever get new servants. Baba becomes furious and says that he will never replace Ali and Hassan. With the start of school, Amir spends hours alone in his room. One afternoon he asks Hassan to walk up the hill with him so he can read him a story. They sit under a pomegranate tree, and Amir asks Hassan what he would do if he threw a pomegranate at him. Amir begins pelting Hassan with pomegranates and yells at Hassan to hit him back. But Hassan won't. He crushes a pomegranate against his own forehead, asks Amir if he is satisfied, and leaves.

That summer of 1976, Amir turns thirteen. Baba invites more than 400 people to the birthday party he plans. At the party Baba makes Amir greet each guest personally. Assef arrives and acts polite as he jokes with Baba. He tells Amir that he chose the gift himself. Amir cannot hide his discomfort, embarrassing Baba and forcing him to apologize. Once Amir is alone he opens the gift, a biography of Hitler, which he throws away. As Amir sits in the dark, Rahim Khan shows up and starts chatting with him, sharing that he was almost married once. The girl was a Hazara. They would meet secretly at night and imagine a life together. But when Rahim Khan told his father, his father became enraged and sent the girl and her family away. Rahim Khan says it was for the best. His family's rejection of her would have been too painful in the long run. He tells Amir he is always there to listen, then gives him a leather-bound notebook for his stories. Fireworks begin, and the two rush back to the house, where Amir sees Hassan serving drinks to Assef and Wali.

Summary: Chapter 9

The next morning Amir opens his presents. He thinks to himself that either he or Hassan must leave. As he is returning from a ride on his new bicycle, Ali stops him and gives him his present. It is a new version of "Shahnamah," the book of stories Amir used to read to Hassan. The morning after, Amir waits for Hassan and Ali to leave the house. He takes his birthday money and a watch that Baba gave him and puts them under Hassan's mattress. He tells Baba that Hassan stole them, and when Ali and Hassan return, Baba asks Hassan if he stole the money and the watch. To Amir's surprise, Hassan says he did. Amir realizes Hassan saw him in the alley, and he also knows that Amir was setting him up now. Baba forgives

Hassan, but Ali says that he and Hassan must leave. Baba pleads with him to stay, but Ali refuses. It rains when Ali and Hassan leave, and Amir watches from inside as they go.

ANALYSIS

Further ironies stemming from Amir's sacrifice of Hassan come to light in this section. Most notably, Amir allowed Hassan to be raped in part because he thought bringing home the kite would win him Baba's love, relieving him of his guilt over his mother's death and making him happy. To some degree he is correct, at least initially. Baba spends more of his time with him, invites him out to a movie when it was always Amir who had to ask, brags about his victory in the kite tournament, and organizes a large party for his birthday. But Amir is unable to fully enjoy these rewards. He is so consumed by a different guilt—guilt over his inaction during Hassan's rape— that he is constantly miserable. During the trip to Jalalabad, he tries to rid himself of this weight. While everyone is sleeping, he says aloud that he saw Hassan raped, hoping someone will hear him. But no one does, and Amir recognizes that his curse is that he is getting away with it. What's more, when he asks Baba if he would ever consider new servants, Baba is so upset, he tells Amir that he is ashamed of him. A similar event occurs at Amir's birthday party, when Baba is embarrassed by Amir's rudeness toward Assef. In other words, Amir's guilt leads him to do things that result in a loss of Baba's approval. Rather than gaining everything he wants, Amir loses the happiness he thought he would have.

Amir does not know how to deal with his feelings of guilt and unhappiness after Hassan's rape. At first he tries to keep away from Hassan, who becomes a constant reminder to Amir of his own cowardice and selfishness. He seems to think avoiding Hassan means he won't feel these things any longer. But Hassan is a part of the household, so Amir can never escape him completely. When the two are face to face, Amir wishes Hassan would punish him. He pelts Hassan with the pomegranates, for instance, because he wants Hassan to hit him back. Punishment, Amir feels, would at least begin to make up for the way he wronged Hassan. Hassan, however, will not retaliate, and this becomes the greatest torment for Amir. Hassan proves that his love and loyalty are unshakable, whereas Amir proves that his love and loyalty are weak. One of Amir's constant fears is realized: Hassan emerges as the stronger, better person. Amir cannot tolerate this truth and engineers a plan to make Ali and Hassan leave. Yet his guilt is only heightened when Hassan admits to stealing the money and watch. Amir recognizes that Hassan is sacrificing himself again, despite knowing that Amir did not do the same for him when he was raped.

There are also more examples in this section of the injustices against Hazaras. When Rahim Khan's father becomes angry because Rahim Khan wants to marry a Hazara woman, he resolves the problem not by moving his own family, but by sending away the Hazara woman and her family. Similarly, to resolve the tension between Hassan and Amir, Ali decides that they will leave. Both the Hazara family from Rahim Khan's story and Ali and Hassan go to Hazarajat, an isolated, mountainous region in central Afghanistan that is principally inhabited by Hazaras. But perhaps the most poignant image of the injustice toward Hazaras is the moment Amir witnesses Hassan serving drinks to Assef and Wali from a silver platter. Hassan cannot do anything about the rape because of his inferior status as a poor Hazara, and Assef, whose family is rich and powerful, knows it. Hassan dutifully serves Assef, the boy who raped him, and Assef expresses no remorse or shame during the encounter. Instead, he grins at Hassan and kneads him in the chest tauntingly with his knuckle.

CHAPTERS 10–11

SUMMARY: CHAPTER 10
It is March 1981. Amir and Baba are in the back of a truck with several other Afghans on the way to Pakistan. The ride makes Amir sick, and he worries he is embarrassing Baba. Because they can't trust anyone, they left home in the middle of the night. The *rafiqs*, or comrades, as Amir calls them, have divided society. People turn each other in for money or under threat. The truck driver, Karim, has a business arrangement with the soldiers guarding the road. But when they arrive at the checkpoint, the Russian guard eyes a woman in the truck and says the price of passing is half an hour with her. Baba won't allow it. The Russian threatens to shoot Baba and raises his handgun, but another Russian officer stops him. After they pass the checkpoint, the husband of the woman kisses Baba's hand. When they arrive in Jalalabad, where they are to switch trucks, Karim tells them that the truck they need broke the previous week. Baba becomes enraged and attacks Karim for not telling them earlier.

For a week they stay in a basement with other refugees. Amir recognizes Kamal, who looks sickly and depressed, and Kamal's father. Amir overhears Kamal's father telling Baba what happened to Kamal that made him so weak. Four men caught Kamal out alone, and when he came back to his father he was bleeding "down there" (p. 120). Kamal no longer speaks, just stares. Finally Karim finds a truck to take them to Pakistan. It's a fuel truck, and the air inside is thick with fumes, making it difficult to breathe. They arrive in Pakistan, but once they're out of the truck Kamal's father begins screaming. Kamal has stopped breathing. Kamal's father attacks Karim, wrestling Karim's gun away. Before anyone can act, Kamal's father puts the gun in his own mouth and shoots.

SUMMARY: CHAPTER 11

The story jumps forward in time. Baba and Amir are in Fremont, California, where they have lived for nearly two years. Baba, who works at a gas station now, has had difficulty adjusting to life in the U.S. One day, in a convenience store he often shops at, he overturns a magazine rack because the manager asks for ID when Baba tries to pay with a check. Amir wants to explain that, in Afghanistan, everyone trusted each other to pay. That night Amir asks if it's best that they return to Pakistan. Baba says they're in America for Amir, who is about to finish high school and go to college. On the night of Amir's graduation, Baba takes him out for a big dinner, then to a bar where he buys drinks all night. He also gives Amir an old Ford Grand Torino as a gift. In the days after, Amir tells Baba that he wants to study writing. Baba disapproves and says the degree will be useless, but Amir has made up his mind.

Amir describes the drives he takes in his car. He passes through rundown and rich neighborhoods, and talks about the first time he saw the ocean. For Amir, America is a place to forget the past. The next summer, in 1984, Baba buys an old van. On Saturday mornings, he and Amir go to garage sales, loading the van with their purchases, then on Sundays set up a booth at the flea market and sell everything for a profit. One morning Baba speaks with a man whom he introduces to Amir as General Taheri. Baba tells General Taheri that Amir is going to be a great writer. General Taheri's daughter, Soraya, comes over, and she and Amir make eye contact. On the drive home Amir asks Baba about her. All Baba knows is that she was romantically involved with a man once, but it didn't end well. Amir falls asleep that night thinking of her.

ANALYSIS

The first half of the section primarily describes Baba and Amir's horrific journey, first to Jalalabad and finally to Peshawar, Pakistan. It also gives some detail about how Kabul has changed in the roughly five years that have elapsed since chapter 9. In April 1978, the Communists left in Afghanistan overthrew President Daoud Khan. The coup created a split in Afghan society that led to numerous executions and widespread fear. Regular Afghans were encouraged or forced to turn in anyone who might be an enemy of the ruling faction. It turned out to be the first in a series of events that led to an invasion by Russia at the end of 1979, plunging the country into even greater turmoil. Baba and Amir flee from this atmosphere and the Russian occupation at the opening of the section.

To Baba, for whom doing the right thing is so important, the loss of honor and decency in Afghanistan is perhaps the greatest tragedy to befall his country. The atrocities described, including the Russian guard's attempted rape of the woman in the truck and the rape of Kamal that is implied, are examples of how the rule of law has essentially collapsed. Though the war has forced Baba and Amir to leave their home and nearly all their possessions behind, Baba only believes more strongly in the necessity of acting with dignity and doing what is right. As he declares to the Russian guard, decency becomes even more important during times of war. This is in large part why Baba becomes furious at Karim when he discovers that Karim has lied and there is no truck waiting to take them to Pakistan, and it is what motivates him to risk his life to preserve the dignity of a woman he doesn't even know. He is trying to preserve the honor of not just one person, but of all of Afghanistan. The episode is another instance of the overarching theme of the rape of Afghanistan's powerless by those in power.

The move to America represents two completely different things to Amir and Baba. In California, Baba feels disconnected from everything he knows. In Kabul, he would send Amir and Hassan to the baker with a stick. The baker would make a notch in the stick for each loaf of bread he gave, and at the end of the month, Baba paid the baker according to how many notches there were. When the manager at the convenience store asks Baba for ID, Baba feels insulted because he takes it as a sign of distrust. He doesn't recognize that it is a normal question in the U.S. Baba has also lost social status. In Kabul, he was wealthy and respected. In California, he earns low wages working at a gas station. Amir makes a particularly ironic comment, remarking that some of the homes he sees make Baba's house in Kabul look like a servant's hut. In the past, Ali and Hassan were the servants, and Baba was the master. Now Baba is more like a servant himself. These differences leave Baba perpetually frustrated. In small ways, he continues trying to reclaim the life he had in Kabul, as when he buys everyone drinks the night of Amir's graduation.

Amir also feels disconnected from everything he knew in Kabul, but for him this disconnection has a different meaning. He sees it as an opportunity for a new beginning, and he thinks of America as a place where he can literally escape his past. Most significantly, it is a place where he doesn't have to be reminded of Hassan and the rape. The metaphor Amir chooses to describe America is of a river. The metaphor has two meanings that are related but separate. First, a river always moves forward. In other words, it is always moving toward the future and never toward the past. Second, the river is a common symbol for washing away sin. In Christianity, for instance, baptism symbolizes purification and regeneration. Amir similarly wants a new birth, free of the sins he committed in letting Hassan be raped, and lying to force Hassan and Ali out of Baba's house.

CHAPTERS 12–13

SUMMARY: CHAPTER 12

After nearly a year of longing for Soraya, Amir finally gets the nerve to speak to her. General Taheri is away, but while they're talking, Soraya's mother, Jamila—whom Amir addresses formally as Khanum Taheri at first—returns. She asks Amir to sit, but he does the proper Afghan thing and declines. For weeks he talks to Soraya only when General Taheri is away, until one day as he is giving her one of the stories he wrote, General Taheri arrives. General Taheri throws the story into a garbage can and, walking Amir away, tells him to remember that he is among other Afghans, *all* of whom are storytellers. Amir is disheartened, but he soon becomes focused on Baba, who is ill. Baba is diagnosed with lung cancer but refuses to receive treatment. Amir tells Baba he doesn't know what he's supposed to do. Baba replies that he's been trying to teach Amir precisely this all his life and forbids Amir to tell anyone about his illness.

As the months pass, Baba weakens until one day he collapses. The cancer has spread to his brain. Afghans arrive in droves to see Baba in the hospital. After his father is discharged, Amir asks him to go to General Taheri to ask for Soraya's hand in marriage for Amir. Baba goes happily the next day. General Taheri accepts, and after Baba tells Amir over the phone, he puts Soraya on the line. Soraya is happy, but says she must tell Amir about her past because she doesn't want any secrets. When she was eighteen, she ran away with an Afghan man. They lived together for nearly a month before General Taheri found her and took her home. While she was gone, her mother had a stroke. Amir admits it bothers him a little, but he still wants to marry her.

SUMMARY: CHAPTER 13

The following night, Amir and Baba go to the Taheris' home for the traditional ceremony of "giving word." General Taheri is happy and says they are doing it the right way now. Because Baba is so sick, they plan to have the wedding soon. Baba rents an Afghan banquet hall for the ceremony, buys the ring, Amir's tuxedo, and other necessities, until he has spent almost all of his $35,000 savings. Of the wedding, Amir remembers sitting on a sofa with Soraya. They are covered with a veil and look at each other's reflections in a mirror. It is the first time he tells her he loves her, and they are together for the first time that night. Shortly after, Baba dies. Many Afghans whom Baba helped come to the funeral. As he listens to them pay their respects, Amir realizes how Baba defined who he was.

Because their engagement was so brief, Amir doesn't learn about Soraya's family until after the wedding. General Taheri does not work. He feels it is below him and keeps the family on welfare. He also does not allow Jamila, who was once a great singer, to sing in public. Soraya tells Amir that, on the night her father brought her home after she ran away, he arrived with a gun, and once she was home he made her cut off her hair. Amir is different from every Afghan guy she has ever met.

In the summer of 1988, Amir finishes his first novel. He gets it published, and then he and Soraya start trying to have a baby. They are unable to conceive, however, and after numerous tests, doctors cannot explain why they can't have a child. They talk about adoption, but General Taheri says he doesn't like the idea. Amir agrees, though he doesn't seem certain. Amir's writing career has gone well in the meantime, and with the advance from his second novel, he and Soraya buy a house in San Francisco. But the inability to have a child still lingers between them.

ANALYSIS

The different events of this section all revolve around one focus: Amir becoming a man. He marries and makes love for the first time. He loses Baba and becomes fully responsible for himself. He also completes and publishes his first novel, establishing his career as a writer. In all of these events, Amir experiences a profound mix of joy and pain. Embracing independence and adulthood also require letting go of his childhood dependence on Baba. When Amir pleads with Baba to try chemotherapy, Amir asks what he is supposed to do without Baba. Baba replies that this is what he has been trying to teach Amir his whole life. To Amir, it is clear for the first time why Baba has always treated him the way he has. He was preparing Amir to take care of himself and to know right from wrong. In other words, he was teaching Amir to be a man. In his transition to adulthood, Amir also transitions from one family to another. At the beginning of the section he is a boy living in his father's house. At the end, he is a man with a wife and his own home. What Baba does witness of this makes him happy, and he dies proud of Amir. Only one crucial thing remains missing for Amir. He wants to have a child.

Despite Amir's growth into an adult, one part of his childhood he does not let go of. He still feels guilty about Hassan. This guilt, though not as prominent as it once was, still rises to the surface on occasion. Sometimes Amir simply wonders about him, as when he wonders if Hassan has married. Other times his guilt is more pronounced. When Soraya tells Amir about the time she ran away with another man, Amir actually feels jealous that she is able to speak about the incident. For Soraya, her secret is an event in the past that is over and done with. For Amir, however, his secret is very much still present, and he still cannot talk about it. Amir feels that until he is able to atone for his treatment of Hassan, it will continue to haunt him.

Another subject of the section is the way the Afghan refugees, Amir and Baba included, preserve their culture in California. In the U.S., no controversy results from a young man and woman speaking in public without adults present. For Afghans, however, such encounters are not entirely appropriate. Certain customs must be followed. General Taheri feels the need to remind Amir of this fact when he sees Amir speaking with Soraya. He tells Amir he is among Afghan peers. The message is clear: they may be in California, but Afghanistan is still present, and Amir should act accordingly. From that point forward Amir's courtship of Soraya proceeds in a more traditional fashion. Amir does not propose to Soraya, for instance. Baba is the one who proposes the marriage to General Taheri. The wedding takes place in an Afghan banquet hall, and the ceremony follows Afghan customs, such as Amir and Soraya gazing at each other's reflection in a mirror while they are covered with a veil.

Traditional Afghan culture is not always positive, however, and the section slips in some comments on the way it treats women. For instance, General Taheri, who is portrayed as the paradigm of Afghan manhood, does not allow Jamila to sing in public, despite the fact that she was once famous in Kabul for her beautiful voice. Even Jamila, who knows firsthand the limits the culture places on women, exhibits this way of thinking. She dotes on Amir compulsively just because he married Soraya. Amir says he could go on a killing spree and she would still approve of him, because without Amir, Soraya might have aged alone, and every woman needs a husband. Implicit here is a belief that a woman needs a man if she is to lead a meaningful life. A double standard exists in the way Afghan society treats men and women regarding sex. Soraya complains that she lost value when she ran away because she was no longer considered virtuous. Men, meanwhile, can have sex with anyone and will be viewed as guys who are just having fun. Amir does not have these prejudices. He attributes this to the fact that Baba was a liberal Afghan, but also because he grew up without women around, so he was never exposed to this double standard.

CHAPTERS 14–15

SUMMARY: CHAPTER 14

The period is June 2001, and Amir has just received a call from Rahim Khan, who wants Amir to see him in Pakistan. Amir tells Soraya he has to go. Rahim Khan, the first grownup Amir ever thought of as a friend, is very ill. Amir takes a walk to Golden Gate Park, and as he sits watching a man play catch with his son and looking at the kites flying, he thinks of something Rahim Khan said to him on the phone. He told Amir there was a way for him to be good again. That night, while Amir and Soraya are in bed, Amir thinks of their relationship. They still make love, but both of them feel a kind of futility in the act. They used to lie together and talk about having a child, but now their conversations are about work or other things. Amir drifts off to sleep and dreams of Hassan running through the snow. A week later, Amir leaves for Pakistan.

SUMMARY: CHAPTER 15

Amir lands in Peshawar, where Rahim Khan is. The driver of the cab he takes talks incessantly, telling Amir that what has happened to Afghanistan is awful. They reach the neighborhood known as "Afghan Town," and Amir sees carpet shops, kabob vendors, and dirty children selling cigarettes. Amir remembers the last time he saw Rahim Khan, twenty years earlier in 1981. It was the night he and Baba left Kabul. They had gone to see Rahim Khan, and Baba had cried. Baba and Rahim Khan had kept in touch, but Amir had not spoken with Rahim Khan since just after Baba's death.

Amir arrives at Rahim Khan's apartment, and Rahim Khan answers the door. He looks thin and sickly. Inside they have tea and they talk. Amir tells him he is married now to Soraya Taheri, General Taheri's daughter, and he talks about Baba and about his own career as a novelist. Rahim Khan says he never doubted that Amir would become a writer. The conversation turns to what Afghanistan has become since the Taliban took over. Rahim Khan tells Amir the story of how he got the scar over his eye. A man next to him at a soccer game cheered loudly. The guard on patrol heard the noise, walked over, and smashed Rahim Khan with the butt of his rifle. Amir learns that Rahim Khan had been living in Baba's house in Kabul since 1981, when Amir and Baba fled. He took care of the place, as Baba expected to eventually return. Meanwhile, Kabul became dangerous, as the fighting between Afghan factions vying for control of the city grew worse. Rockets fell randomly, destroying homes and killing civilians. Rahim Khan says he cheered at first when the Taliban took over and ended the fighting.

Rahim Khan coughs blood into a napkin while they're speaking, and Amir asks how well he is. Rahim Khan replies that he is dying and does not expect to live through the summer. He says that he asked Amir there because he wanted to see him, but also because he wanted something else. In the years he lived in Baba's house, he was not alone. Hassan was with him. Before he asks Amir for the favor, he says he must tell him about Hassan.

ANALYSIS

The call Amir receives from Rahim Khan at the beginning of the section is the same one he refers to in the book's first chapter. The narrative has almost come back to the present, though some important events need to occur before that happens completely. Amir has not spoken to Rahim Khan for twenty years, and hearing from him visibly shakes Amir. He is upset to hear that Rahim Khan is ill, but the call upsets him for another reason, which becomes clear when he takes his walk to Golden Gate Park and watches the kites flying. He realizes that Rahim Khan knows about everything that happened with Hassan, evident in Rahim Khan's comment to Amir that he knows of a way for Amir to be good again. Amir is again reminded of his treatment of Hassan, and despite the life Amir has made for himself in California, he will not be free of this guilt until he finds a way to make up for letting Hassan be raped and then falsely accusing Hassan of stealing from him.

Though Amir does not yet know how to atone for his sins against Hassan, two hints about how he will do it occur in the section. The only things keeping Amir from being completely happy are his guilt and the fact that he and Soraya are unable to have a child. For Amir, these have become linked into one feeling of emptiness. To underscore the way Amir links the two, as he lies in bed with Soraya he thinks first of their inability to have a baby, then dreams of Hassan running in the snow. Amir's narration implies that he goes to see Rahim Khan in Pakistan not only because Rahim Khan is sick but also because, as Rahim Khan says, he knows a way for Amir to be good again. Amir hopes there will finally be some way for him to correct the wrong that lingers in his thoughts.

Once he arrives in Pakistan, Amir begins to realize the extent of what has happened to the people of Afghanistan and the events that have destroyed Kabul in the time he has been away. When the cab driver takes him through "Afghan Town," for instance, Amir sees children covered in dirt and selling cigarettes along the road, indicating that they are poor. Although they were forced to leave everything behind, Amir and Baba were lucky in the sense that they were able to make it to the United States and to some degree rebuild their lives. Many of the Afghans who had to flee had little to begin with, and wound up with even less as refugees. Amir sees sights familiar from Afghanistan, like the carpet shops and kabob vendors, mixed with the degradation the Afghans now endure. The smells he describes as he passes through Afghan Town, which include the familiar aroma of a food called *pakora* mixed with poverty, signifying stench of "rot, garbage, and feces" (p. 196), represent this combination.

Based on Rahim Khan's description, it's evident that the fighting destroyed everything, from the buildings Amir knew to the way of life he remembers in Kabul. Rahim Khan says the Alliance did more to ruin the city than the Shorawi did. The Alliance he refers to is the Northern Alliance, a militia made up of different non-Pashtun ethnic groups. The Northern Alliance was one of the militias that helped to push the Soviets, or Shorawi, out of Kabul and ultimately out of Afghanistan. But once the Soviets were gone, these militias began fighting each other for control of Kabul and the country, resulting in a great deal of damage and numerous civilian deaths. Rahim Khan mentions Gulbuddin, or Gulbuddin Hekmatyar, who led one of the factions that caused the most destruction in Kabul. It was the Taliban that ultimately emerged in control. Initially they quelled the fighting, so Afghans like Rahim Khan rejoiced. But they quickly implemented a rigid code of Islamic law and maintained order through brute force. Rather than end the nightmare the Afghans had lived with, the Taliban prolonged it.

CHAPTERS 16–17

SUMMARY: CHAPTER 16
Rahim Khan tells Amir the story of how he found Hassan, and the narrative shifts so that Rahim Khan narrates in the first person. In 1986, Rahim Khan went to Hazarajat. He went primarily because he was lonely, but also because as he aged it became difficult for him to care for Baba's house by himself. He found Hassan's home, a small mud house, and saw Hassan in the yard. The men greeted each other, and Hassan took Rahim Khan inside to introduce him to his wife, a pregnant Hazara woman named Farzana. As they spoke, Rahim Khan learned that Ali was killed by a land mine. Rahim Khan then explained to Hassan that he wanted Hassan and Farzana to come to Baba's house with him and help him care for it. Hassan declined, saying that Hazarajat was their home now. Hassan asked several questions about Amir. When he learned Baba was dead, he cried. Rahim Khan stayed the night, and in the morning, Hassan told him that he and Farzana would go back to Kabul.

Out of respect, Hassan and Farzana live in the small servants' hut on Baba's property, and Hassan works diligently cleaning and repairing the house. That fall, Farzana gives birth to a stillborn girl, whom they bury in the yard. Farzana becomes pregnant again in 1990, and that same year Sanaubar, Hassan's mother, appears at the front gate, weak and with her face severely cut up. Hassan and Farzana nurse her back to health, and she and Hassan become close. That winter it is Sanaubar who delivers Hassan and Farzana's son.

Sanaubar loves and cares for the boy, who is named Sohrab, after the character from Hassan and Amir's favorite childhood story. Sanaubar lives until Sohrab is four. By then it is 1995. The Soviets had been pushed out of Kabul, but fighting continues between rival Afghan groups. Hassan, meanwhile, is teaching Sohrab to read and to run kites. In 1996, the Taliban take control of Kabul. Two weeks later they ban kite fighting.

SUMMARY: CHAPTER 17

The story shifts back to Amir's perspective. Amir sits with Rahim Khan thinking of everything that happened between Hassan and himself. Amir asks if Hassan is still in Baba's house, and Rahim Khan hands him an envelope. It contains a photograph of Hassan and a letter for Amir. In it, Hassan says the Kabul they used to know is gone. One day a man at the market hit Farzana simply because she raised her voice so another man who was half-deaf could hear her. He talks about his love for his son, and says Rahim Khan is very ill. If Amir ever returns, he will find his faithful friend Hassan waiting for him. Rahim Khan says a month after arriving in Pakistan, he received a call from a neighbor in Kabul. The Taliban had gone to Baba's house and found Hassan and his family there. Hassan said he was taking care of the house for a friend, and they called him a liar like all Hazaras. They made him kneel in the street and shot him in the head. When Farzana ran out of the house, they shot her too.

The Taliban moved into Baba's house, and Sohrab was sent to an orphanage. Rahim Khan knows an American couple in Pakistan that care for Afghan orphans, and they have already agreed to take in Sohrab. Amir says he can't go to Kabul. He can pay someone else to get Sohrab. Rahim Khan says it is not about the money and that Amir knows why he must go. Rahim Khan says that one day Baba told him he was worried that a boy who can't stand up for himself becomes a man who can't stand up to anything. He tells Amir one more thing. Ali was unable to have children. Amir asks who Hassan's father was then, and Rahim Khan says Amir knows. Hassan never knew. They couldn't tell anyone because it was a shameful situation. Amir shouts at Rahim Khan and storms out of the apartment.

ANALYSIS

The events of this section, which largely recount what happened to Hassan in the time since Baba and Amir left for Pakistan, deftly tie together several of the book's thematic elements: the pain of guilt, the hatefulness of racial prejudice, the challenge of acting against injustice, the value of loyalty, the love as well as the discord between fathers and sons, and the role history plays in private lives. We do not learn all the details of Hassan's life, but we learn the basics. Most importantly, we now know that he had a son, Sohrab. In many ways, Hassan's relationship with Sohrab acts as indirect proof that Hassan never forgot Amir. Naming the boy after a character in his and Amir's favorite story is one example. Hassan also did with Sohrab all the things he and Amir used to enjoy, such as going to the movies and flying kites. The relationship between Hassan and Sohrab also adds a new dimension to the theme of fathers and sons that runs through the novel. It is perhaps the most loving father-son relationship we see in the book, making it all the more painful when we learn that Hassan is dead.

Hassan's murder is important for many reasons. It plays multiple roles in the section, and in the novel as a whole. For instance, it brings together two of the story's major themes. His death is presented as a combination of the political strife ravaging Kabul and the entrenched prejudice against Hazaras that has turned up repeatedly in the novel. Two members of the Taliban, who at this point control Kabul without competition, shoot Hassan. Rahim Khan's telling of the story implies that these Taliban officials want Baba's house, and since Hassan is a Hazara, he essentially has no rights. Conspicuously, the men are not punished for killing Hassan and Farzana. The suggestion is that, to these men, the lives of Hazaras have no value, or at least not enough value to punish anyone for ending them. Foreshadowing of Hassan's death occurs when the Taliban first take over Kabul. Though most of the city's residents celebrate the event, Hassan does not cheer. "God help the Hazaras now," he says to Rahim Khan at the end of chapter 16 (p. 213).

Hassan's death also marks a turning point in Amir's quest for redemption. To Amir, the news of Hassan's murder means not only that he has lost his friend forever, but also that he can never apologize to Hassan for allowing his rape and then lying about him stealing his birthday money. Making up for these actions was part of the reason he traveled to Pakistan in the first place. Initially, the story suggests that Amir will have to live with his guilt permanently, but Rahim Khan says that one way remains for him to make amends. Amir can go to Kabul, find Sohrab, and bring him back to Pakistan, where he can be taken care of. The request is not Rahim Khan's alone. Hassan said in his letter to Amir that the most important thing for him was to survive, so that Sohrab would not become an orphan. With Hassan and Farzana dead and Rahim Khan ill, Amir is perhaps the only person who can make sure Sohrab is not abandoned.

Going to Kabul becomes a test of Amir's honor, loyalty, and manhood. Amir is clearly afraid to go. He knows the city is extremely dangerous, and in returning there he would risk everything he has, including his life and the welfare of his family. Kabul will also undoubtedly recall memories of Hassan and his past that Amir would rather not confront. Rahim Khan recognizes that the decision is a difficult one for Amir. To convince him, he brings up the conversation he once had with Baba, when Baba said he feared that Amir would not be able to stand up to anything as a man if he could not stand up for himself as a boy. Amir concedes that Baba may have been right. Then Rahim Khan reveals that Ali was not Hassan's father, and implies that Hassan was, in fact, Baba's child. Hassan and Amir, then, would be half brothers, and Sohrab would be Amir's nephew, obligating Amir further to find the boy. The dilemma brings together the tensions Amir has struggled with in the novel. By rescuing Sohrab, Amir can become the man that Baba always wanted him to be and he can finally atone for the ways he failed Hassan as a friend.

CHAPTERS 18–19

SUMMARY: CHAPTER 18

Amir walks from Rahim Khan's house to a small teahouse, thinking about how he was responsible for Hassan's death. He also goes over the evidence that Baba was Hassan's father: Baba's paying for the surgery to fix Hassan's lip and his weeping when Ali and Hassan left. Baba had said that theft was the only sin, and Amir thinks how Baba stole from him a brother, from Hassan his identity, from Ali his honor. Amir realizes he and Baba were more alike than he knew. They had both betrayed their truest friends. What Rahim Khan wants is for Amir to atone for Baba's sins and his own. On the ride back to Rahim Khan's, Amir recognizes he is not too old to start fighting for himself, and that somewhere in Kabul a small part of Hassan remains. He finds Rahim Khan praying and tells him he will find Sohrab.

SUMMARY: CHAPTER 19

Rahim Khan arranges for an acquaintance named Farid to take Amir to Kabul. Farid and his father had fought against the Soviets. Later, after Farid had children, he lost two daughters and three fingers on his left hand to a land mine. Amir is dressed in an Afghan hat called a *pakol* and wears a fake beard that reaches down to his chest. Once in Afghanistan Amir says he feels like a tourist in his own country. Farid asks sarcastically if, after twenty years in America, Amir still thinks of Afghanistan as his country. He guesses that Amir grew up in a large house with servants, that his father drove an American car, and that Amir has never worn a *pakol* before. He points to an old man in ragged clothing and says that is the real Afghanistan. Amir has always been a tourist there.

They stop for the night at the home of Farid's brother, Wahid. The house is small, with bare dirt walls and two lamps for light. Inside, Wahid's wife and another woman bring tea. The three men talk for a time, and Wahid asks Amir why he has returned to Afghanistan. Farid says contemptuously that Amir is probably coming to sell his land and run with the money back to America. Wahid snaps at Farid for insulting a guest in his home, but Amir says he should have explained earlier. He is going to find a Hazara boy, his illegitimate half brother, so that he can take him to Peshawar where people will take care of him. Wahid calls Amir a true Afghan and says he is proud to have Amir stay in his home.

Wahid's wife serves dinner to Farid and Amir, and Wahid says he and his family ate earlier. While Amir eats, he notices Wahid's three boys staring at his wristwatch. He gives the boys the watch as a gift, though they lose interest quickly. As Amir and Farid lie down to sleep, Farid says it was wrong of him to assume Amir's reason for returning and says he will help Amir find the boy. That night, Amir dreams of a man shooting Hassan, and realizes he is the man in the dream. He goes outside to think and hears two voices coming from the house, Wahid's and his wife's. They are arguing about dinner. Because they gave Amir their food, the children did not have any dinner. Amir realizes that the boys weren't staring at his watch, they were staring at his food. The next morning, before Amir and Farid leave, Amir stuffs a wad of money under one of their mattresses.

ANALYSIS

Another irony appears in this section: Amir realizes he is more like Baba than he thought. However, what they share is betrayal of their best friends. Baba betrayed Ali, his closest friend since childhood, by sleeping with Sanaubar. As Amir says, having sex with a man's wife is the worst possible way an Afghan man can be dishonored. Amir similarly betrayed Hassan. But despite all Baba's lies, Amir sees that Baba was correct to say that Amir always let someone else fight his battles for him. Though Amir never says so explicitly, he knows he is doing what Baba would have done in the situation when he resolves to go to Kabul to find Sohrab. The situation presents a further twist of irony in that Amir realizes he can share in Baba's greatest virtue, the courage to do what is right, only after he has recognized that he shares Baba's greatest failing as well. If Amir saves Sohrab, both he and Baba will be pardoned, at least to some degree, for the ways they betrayed their dearest and closest friends.

Amir's guilt over the way he treated Hassan also plays a significant role in his decision to return to Kabul. As Amir leaves Rahim Khan's house, Amir wonders if the chain of events that followed from his coercing Hassan and Ali out of Baba's house eventually led to Ali stepping on a landmine and to Hassan being shot. Had Amir acted differently, Ali and Hassan never would have left for Hazarajat, and both might still be alive now. Through this logic, Amir has made himself responsible for their deaths. He realizes he cannot save them, but a piece of Hassan lives on in Sohrab. By rescuing Sohrab, Amir will figuratively rescue Hassan as well. With this in mind, and the knowledge that he still has time to begin fighting for himself, Amir returns to Rahim Khan's house to tell him he will make the trip back to Afghanistan.

As Amir returns to Kabul, he is confronted by some of the unpleasant realities he left behind in Afghanistan, many of which are embodied by Amir's driver, Farid. While Amir was in the United States attending school, countless Afghans were fighting to free their country from the Soviets. Thousands of Afghan men died, leaving children behind. After these wars, landmines that had been planted to kill the enemy were never cleared. As a result, children were frequently killed or injured by mines hidden in land that hadn't seen fighting in years. Farid knows all these facts firsthand. He lost his father to the fighting when he was sixteen, then later lost two daughters as well as some fingers and toes to a landmine blast. Though Amir left behind his wealthy life when he and Baba left Afghanistan, he still never had to endure the tragedies that the average Afghan faced during the 1980s and 90s. Farid recognizes that Amir did not suffer the way many Afghans did. Amir escaped when Farid and most others could not, making Farid resent Amir at first.

Farid's other reason for treating Amir contemptuously has to do with class. While rich Afghans had the money to leave, an expensive endeavor that required paying drivers to smuggle them out or buying plane tickets, most Afghans did not. Even before the wars destroyed Afghanistan, life was different for the rich. Knowing that Amir grew up rich, Farid says Amir was always a tourist in Afghanistan. As a boy, Amir lived in a large house with servants. Most Afghans, by contrast, had very little. When Farid points to the old man walking with a sack filled with scrub grass on his back and calls him the real Afghanistan, he is right to a large degree, and Amir knows it. Even Amir's job as a writer represents a privileged life, which is why he is slightly embarrassed to tell Wahid what he does. Amir's most troubling confrontation with Afghanistan's poverty occurs when he overhears Wahid and his wife arguing. He realizes they gave him their food out of courtesy, but it meant that they and their children had nothing to eat. In an act recalling the way he framed Hassan years earlier, he stuffs money under the mattress before he leaves, only this time he does it to make amends.

CHAPTERS 20–21

SUMMARY: CHAPTER 20

On the way to Kabul, Amir sees signs of the wars, such as broken-down Soviet tanks and destroyed villages. When Amir and Farid reach Kabul, Amir does not recognize it. What used to be buildings are now dusty piles of rubble, and beggars are everywhere. The trees are all gone. The Soviets cut them down because snipers would hide in them, and Afghans cut them down to use for firewood. A Taliban patrol of bearded men with guns in the back of a red pickup passes by, and Amir stares at them. Farid rebukes Amir, saying the Taliban will use any excuse for violence, and an old beggar speaks up in agreement with Farid. The beggar, it turns out, was a literature professor and once knew Sofia Akram, Amir's mother. Amir asks him several questions about her, but soon has to leave.

Amir and Farid find the orphanage where they think Sohrab is. The director, Zaman, is cautious and doesn't admit that he has seen Sohrab until Amir says he is Sohrab's half uncle. The orphanage itself was once a storage warehouse for a carpet manufacturer. There are hundreds of children and not enough beds, mattresses, or blankets. That past winter, one child froze to death. Zaman says Sohrab is not there, but he knows where he may be. It might already be too late, however. Amir asks what he means, and Zaman tells him there is a Taliban official who comes every month or two. The official brings cash, and will sometimes take a child with him. Farid attacks Zaman for letting this occur, but stops when he notices children in view. Zaman says he can do nothing against the Taliban, and it is the only way to get money to feed the children. He tells Amir and Farid that the official took Sohrab a month ago. If they want to find him, he will be at Ghazi Stadium the next day.

Summary: Chapter 21

Farid drives Amir to Baba's house. It is falling apart, but recognizable. Amir finds his bedroom window and remembers looking out of it to watch Ali and Hassan the morning they left. He goes up the hill to the pomegranate tree where he and Hassan used to play, but Farid tells him they should leave. That night they stay at a dilapidated hotel. The following day they go to the soccer game at Ghazi Stadium. The field is just dirt, and the crowd is careful not to cheer too loudly. At halftime, Taliban in red pickups drive into the stadium. They unload a blindfolded man from one truck and a blindfolded woman from the other and bury each up to the chest in a hole on the field. The woman is screaming uncontrollably.

A cleric on the field recites a prayer from the Koran and announces that they are there to carry out God's law. When adulterers throw stones at the house of God, he shouts, they must answer by throwing stones back. Another man steps out of a pickup, and Farid and Amir see it is the official they are looking for. He is wearing black sunglasses, as Zaman said. The official throws stones at the head of the man in the hole until his head is a bloody pulp and his chin hangs to his chest. Then he does the same to the woman. They pile the bodies into the back of a truck, and the second half of the soccer game begins. Farid tells one of the Taliban nearby that he has personal business with the official, and the official agrees to see them that afternoon.

Analysis

As Amir and Farid look for Sohrab, the reader sees through Amir's eyes more of the devastation of Kabul. The city is now completely unfamiliar to Amir, and he looks at it almost as a tourist, as Farid called Amir in the previous section. His description sounds at times like science fiction. Littered with rubble, populated by beggars, the city has become a post apocalyptic nightmare. In a scene that vividly represents Afghanistan's desperation, Farid points out to Amir one man trying to sell his prosthetic leg to another man, who haggles with him over the price. There are few real signs of life left, made clear by the fact that not even trees remain, rendering the landscape oddly desolate. When Amir finds the pomegranate tree where he and Hassan used to play, he discovers it no longer bears fruit. The barren tree serves as a powerful symbol that the Kabul Amir knew is dead, at least figuratively if not yet literally. The city appears even stranger and sadder by the many reminders that this is, in fact, the place where Amir grew up. Amir happens upon the old beggar who knew his mother, for instance, and later finds Baba's house, which has fallen into severe disrepair. As Amir describes his homecoming, it is like bumping into an old friend who has become destitute.

Amir also has his first encounter with the Taliban, the group of Islamic radicals that now control Afghanistan. Farid calls them the "Beard Patrol" as they approach in their red pickup truck. His meaning is double: the term describes the Taliban men, who are all bearded, but it also describes what they are doing, which among other things is to make sure that all men have beards. In Islam's holy texts, men are instructed to let their beards grow to distinguish them from followers of other religions. According to the Taliban, a man who shaves his beard is committing a sin, and they make it their job to punish any person caught sinning. Shaving was one of many illegal acts under the Taliban, which is why Amir buys a fake beard before entering the country. The Taliban also prohibited women from working, which the director of the orphanage, Zaman, says is part of the reason there are so many children there. When Afghan men died during the wars, their wives were left to care for their children. But since the women could not work, they had no way to feed the kids. Rather than watch them starve, they would leave them at orphanages.

The public stoning that Farid and Amir witness at the stadium is another example of Taliban law. The Taliban claim to enforce Sharia, the law that all Muslims are supposed to follow. Because Islam makes no distinction between religious and nonreligious matters, Sharia governs everything from business ethics to criminal justice, which is why a cleric rather than a judge or some other secular official comes out to speak to the crowd before the stoning begins. Many Muslims, however, believe the Taliban used Sharia as a way to oppress women and justify their violent behavior. The book raises this viewpoint as the crowd prepares to watch the stoning. Farid whispers to Amir, "And they call themselves Muslims" (p. 271). In fact, most of the Muslims Amir speaks with, including Zaman and Rahim Khan, deplore the society the Taliban created, underscoring the point that the Islamic state the Taliban established is not supported by all Muslims.

The book hints at the corruption of the Taliban by having a Taliban official taking girls and boys from the orphanage. We do not know at this point why the official is taking the children, but the unspoken implication is that the official is sexually abusing them. Whatever the case, the official is clearly misusing his position of power. As Zaman, the orphanage director, tells Farid after Farid attacks him, he has not been paid in six months and has already spent his life savings on the orphanage. Without the official's money, he is unable to feed the children in his care. Furthermore, if he protests, the official takes ten children instead of one. Much as Hassan was powerless to do anything against Assef, Zaman is now powerless against the Taliban official, and it is Sohrab, Hassan's orphaned son, who is the victim. Again, it is a case of the powerful in Afghanistan taking advantage of the powerless.

CHAPTERS 22–23

SUMMARY: CHAPTER 22

Amir and Farid arrive at the house where Amir will meet the Taliban official. Farid waits in the car, and two guards lead Amir to the room where he is to wait. Amir thinks to himself it may have been a mistake to stop acting like a coward. The Taliban official enters with some guards. Amir and the official greet each other, then one of the guards tears off Amir's fake beard. The official asks Amir if he enjoyed the show at the stadium. He says it wasn't as good as when they went door-to-door shooting families in their homes. That, he says, was liberating. Amir realizes the official is talking about the massacre of Hazaras in Mazar-i-Sharif, which Amir read about in newspapers.

The official asks what Amir does in America. Amir only answers that he is looking for a boy named Sohrab. The official motions to the guards, and Sohrab enters in a blue silk outfit, bells strapped around his ankles and mascara lining his eyes. The guards make Sohrab dance until the Taliban official orders the guards to leave.

While the official rubs Sohrab's stomach, he asks Amir whatever happened to old Babalu, a name Assef used to call Ali, and Amir realizes that the Taliban official is actually Assef. Stunned, Amir says he will pay him for the boy. Assef replies that money is irrelevant and not why he joined the Taliban. He tells Amir he was once imprisoned, and one evening a guard began kicking him until the blows dislodged a kidney stone that had been causing him severe pain. He felt relief and began laughing. At that moment he knew God was on his side.

Assef says he is on a mission to rid Afghanistan of garbage. Amir calls it ethnic cleansing and says he wants Sohrab. Shoving Sohrab forward, Assef says he and Amir have unfinished business. Assef tells the guards that if Amir exits the room alive, he has earned the right to leave. Then Assef puts on a pair of brass knuckles. Amir remembers little after that. He has flashes of Assef hitting him and of swallowing teeth and blood. Amir remembers laughing while Assef beats him, and of feeling relief. He had looked forward to that, and feels healed for the first time. During the beating, Sohrab tells Assef to stop and holds up his slingshot, and when Assef lunges at him, Sohrab shoots, hitting him in the left eye. Sohrab and Amir run out of the house to where Farid waits with the car. As they drive away, Amir passes out.

SUMMARY: CHAPTER 23

A blur of images follows: a woman named Aisha, a man with a mustache, someone he recognizes. Slipping in and out of consciousness, he imagines Baba wrestling the bear. Amir meets Baba's eyes and realizes he is the one wrestling the bear. He wakes up and discovers he is in the hospital in Peshawar. The people he saw are doctors, and Farid is the man he recognized. Amir's mouth is wired shut. His upper lip is split, the bone of his left eye socket broken, several of his ribs cracked, and his spleen ruptured. Farid and Sohrab are there, and Amir thanks them both. Farid tells Amir that Rahim Khan has gone, but he left a note.

In his note, Rahim Khan says he knew everything that happened with Hassan. Though what Amir did was wrong, he was too hard on himself. He knows Amir suffered because of how Baba treated him, but there was a reason. Because Baba couldn't love Hassan openly, he took it out on Amir, whom Baba thought guiltily of as his socially legitimate half. But real good came from Baba's remorse, Rahim Khan says. The orphanage Baba built, the poor that he fed, were his way of redeeming himself. Rahim Khan also leaves Amir a key to a safe-deposit box with money to cover Amir's expenses. He has little time left, he writes, and Amir should not look for him. The next morning, Amir gives Farid the names of the American couple running the orphanage. Amir spends the day playing cards with Sohrab, who barely speaks. Amir decides Peshawar isn't safe, and when Farid learns there never was an American couple to care for Sohrab, Amir leaves for Islamabad and takes Sohrab with him.

ANALYSIS

The climax of the novel, in which Amir is finally able to atone for his past, occurs in Amir's fight against Assef. In another instance of irony, Amir discovers the Taliban official he must rescue Sohrab from is the same person who raped Hassan all those years ago. Yet the bizarre coincidence also creates a situation in which Amir is able to confront the same scenario that was the source of his guilt more than twenty years earlier. From the way Assef touches Sohrab and what he says to Amir, Amir has no doubt that Assef has been sexually abusing Sohrab. Because Sohrab represents a living piece of Hassan, Assef continues a figurative rape of Hassan. But Amir is now in a position to stop it. He can do what Baba always hoped he would and stand up for what is right. As Rahim Khan put it, it is his way to be good again.

In multiple instances, foreshadowing from earlier in the novel is fulfilled in these chapters. In a confrontation with Assef years earlier, Hassan had threatened to shoot Assef's eye out. In response, Assef said he would get his revenge on Hassan and Amir both. Now, Assef has his revenge against Amir. But Hassan's threat is also carried out vicariously through Sohrab, who shoots out Assef's eye as he saves Amir with his slingshot. Representing the idea of an eye for an eye, Assef gets what he deserves. For Amir, the situation means he can now intervene in Hassan's rape, at least symbolically, by saving Sohrab from further sexual abuse. Though Assef brutally beats Amir, Amir's goal isn't to win the fight. The fact that he did not run is what's important, and as Amir says, in a way he welcomes the beating. It is the punishment he deserved for his actions toward Hassan, but which he never received. It is the reason he feels relief and a sense of healing as Assef beats him, and why he begins laughing.

Amir's laughter establishes a significant parallel between Amir and Assef. Before he challenges Amir to a fight, Assef tells a story about the time he was imprisoned. He says he began to laugh as a guard kicked him because it ended the pain he suffered from his kidney stone. Amir's laughing, though stemming from the relief of a different pain, clearly mirrors Assef's. Moreover, while Amir is in the hospital recovering he describes a dream in which Assef tells him, "We're the same, you and I. You nursed with him, but you're *my* twin." (p.307). In fact, the novel establishes a few similarities between Amir and Assef. Both Amir and Assef are Pashtuns from wealthy, well-connected families, and they shared similar upbringings. They represent a particular part of Afghan society, namely the ruling powers. In his note to Amir, Rahim Khan even tells Amir that Baba thought of him as the socially legitimate part of his life, the part that inherited wealth and with it a freedom from punishment, which made Baba feel guilty.

Hassan, on the other hand, represented the poor and oppressed part of Afghanistan. He was the illegitimate boy whom Baba wanted to love but could never love publicly. In this context, Amir and Hassan act as the different sides of their country—the rich and poor, Sunni and Shia, Pashtun and Hazara, powerful and powerless—who are nonetheless still children of the same father. In allowing Assef to rape Hassan, Amir became complicit in the domination of the powerless by the powerful. Only by intervening on behalf of Sohrab, essentially sacrificing himself as Hassan once sacrificed himself for Amir, does Amir redeem himself. He takes a stand against this domination, and in doing so he is left with a split upper lip, recalling Hassan's cleft lip. In Hassan's case, his cleft lip acted as a kind of mark of his position in society. For Amir it is a symbol of his sacrifice, and it signifies the union of Afghanistan's two halves. Through Amir, Khaled Hosseini subtly suggests that if Afghanistan is to atone for its own guilty history of violence and discrimination, it must redeem itself through a similar stand and a similar sacrifice. It is the way for Afghanistan to be good again.

CHAPTERS 24–25

SUMMARY: CHAPTER 24

Amir and Sohrab arrive in Islamabad. When Amir wakes from a nap, Sohrab is gone. Amir remembers Sohrab's fascination with a mosque they had passed and finds him in the mosque parking lot. They talk a little about their parents, and Sohrab asks if God will put him in hell for what he did to Assef. Amir says Assef deserved more than he got, and Hassan would have been proud of Sohrab for saving Amir's life. Sohrab is glad his parents cannot see him. The sexual abuse he suffered makes him feel dirty and sinful. Amir says he is neither, and asks Sohrab if he wants to live in America with him. For a week Sohrab doesn't give an answer, but one afternoon he asks what San Francisco is like. He says he is scared that Amir or his wife will tire of him. He never wants to go back to an orphanage. Amir promises that won't happen, and after Sohrab agrees to go to America, Amir calls Soraya to explain everything.

The next day, Amir goes to the American embassy. The man there tells Amir the adoption will be almost impossible. Without death certificates, there is no way to prove Sohrab is an orphan. Amir should speak to Omar Faisal, an immigration attorney. Amir and Sohrab see Faisal the next day. He says it will be hard, but there are options. Amir can put Sohrab in an orphanage, file a petition, and wait up to two years for the government to approve the adoption. That night, when Amir tells Sohrab he may have to go back to an orphanage, Sohrab screams that they'll hurt him and cries until he falls asleep in Amir's arms. While he sleeps, Amir talks to Soraya, who tells him that Sharif, a family member who works for the U.S. immigration department, or INS, says there are ways to keep Sohrab in the country once he's in. Amir goes to tell Sohrab and finds him bleeding and unconscious in the bathtub.

SUMMARY: CHAPTER 25

Sohrab is rushed to the emergency room. In the hospital waiting area, Amir uses a sheet as a prayer rug and prays for the first time in more than fifteen years. Eventually he falls asleep in a chair and dreams of Sohrab in the bloody water and the razor blade he used to cut himself. A doctor wakes Amir and tells him that Sohrab lost a great deal of blood, but will live. For several days, Amir stays in the hospital while Sohrab sleeps. When Sohrab awakens, Amir asks how he feels, but Sohrab doesn't answer. Amir reads to him, but Sohrab pays no attention. Sohrab tells Amir he is tired of everything. He wants his old life back and says Amir should have left him in the water. Amir says he was coming to explain that they found a way for Sohrab to go to America. But Sohrab stops speaking entirely.

Amir and Sohrab arrive in San Francisco in August 2001. General Taheri and Jamila come over for dinner, and while Soraya and Jamila set the table, Amir tells General Taheri about the Taliban and Kabul. General Taheri tip toes around the subject of Sohrab at first but finally asks why Amir brought back a Hazara boy. Amir says Baba slept with a servant woman. Their son, Hassan, is now dead. Sohrab is Hassan's son and Amir's nephew. Amir tells General Taheri never to call Sohrab a "Hazara boy" in his presence again. After September 11 and the American bombing of Afghanistan that followed, the names of places in Afghanistan are suddenly well known. Amir and Soraya take jobs helping to run and raise money for a hospital on the Afghan-Pakistani border, and General Taheri is summoned to Afghanistan for a ministry position.

One rainy day in March 2002, Amir takes Sohrab, Soraya, and Kamila to a gathering of Afghans at a park. There is a tent where people are cooking. Sohrab, who is still not speaking, stands out in the rain, but eventually the weather clears. Soraya points out kites flying in the sky. Amir finds a kite seller, and with the new kite he walks over to Sohrab. While Amir checks the string, he talks about Hassan. Then, with the kite ready, he asks Sohrab if he wants to fly it. Sohrab doesn't answer, but as Amir runs, sending the kite into the air, Sohrab follows him. When Amir offers again, Sohrab takes the string. A green kite approaches for a battle, and while Amir prepares Sohrab he notices Sohrab looks alert. He shows Sohrab what used to be Hassan's favorite trick, and quickly they have the other kite on the defensive. In one move, Amir and Sohrab sever the other kite's string, cutting it loose. People cheer around them, and a brief smile appears on Sohrab's face. Amir asks if he should run the kite for Sohrab, and Sohrab nods. "For you, a thousand times over," Amir says (p. 371), and sets off running.

ANALYSIS

The ending of the book is not exactly a happy one, and not all loose ends are tied up neatly. It is not certain that the characters we have come to know will get what they want. It is quite the opposite, in fact, and for Sohrab in particular there are fresh wounds that will leave permanent scars. The near endless abuse he has suffered is manifest in almost everything he does. Because of the physical and sexual abuse Assef and the Taliban inflicted on him, he flinches every time Amir reaches out to touch him. He also bathes for long periods because he feels he is literally dirty as a result of his rape. Because of this abuse, as well as the abandonment he experienced when Hassan and Farzana were murdered, he is so terrified of going back to an orphanage, even temporarily, that he tries to kill himself. After he recovers, he says only that he wants his old life back. He stops speaking entirely, instead withdrawing into himself as if into a protective shell, completely unable to trust or open up to another person. In the pink scars on his wrists, he is left with a permanent mark of his trauma. Like everyone in the novel, he may move beyond the past, but he can never undo it.

Amir's redemption is not perfect either. As his feelings of guilt return in the aftermath of Sohrab's attempted suicide, he feels that, because he was going to break the promise he made never to send Sohrab back to an orphanage, it is his fault Sohrab tried to kill himself. As Amir prays in the hospital waiting room, he thinks the sins he committed against Hassan in the past are being revisited on him now. He is responsible now for Sohrab's attempted suicide, for instance, just as he was responsible for the chain of events that led to Hassan's death. Furthermore, because he once pushed Hassan away when Hassan needed him most, God is now taking Sohrab as punishment. Even the relief from his past feelings is not uplifting and transformative. He knows, for example, that his guilt over his relationship with Baba is gone only because he feels no sting when he thinks Baba may have considered Hassan his true son. "I wondered if that was how forgiveness budded," he writes in chapter 25, "not with the fanfare of epiphany, but with pain gathering its things, packing up, and slipping away unannounced in the middle of the night." (p. 359)

With all this, Khaled Hosseini suggests a general lesson about life: that there are no simple solutions to such emotionally and historically complex problems as those we have seen throughout the novel. In a perfectly just world, Amir would have been able to adopt Sohrab without any difficulty and bring him home to a wonderful new life. For that matter, in a perfectly just world, few of the novel's significant events would have occurred at all. At one point, Amir describes an experience he had at a video store in California. A man was looking at a copy of "The Magnificent Seven," and Amir, who had seen the movie thirteen times, gave away the ending. In such movies, the ending reveals the point of the journey. Does the good guy win or does the bad guy? Does the love affair end tragically or happily? Amir isn't sure exactly how his story ends. Life, he says, is not a movie. Of course, it is Khaled Hosseini, the author, putting these thoughts in the minds of his fictional creations. But in doing so, he proposes something about the goal of fiction. If fiction wants to be true to life, it cannot provide easy answers to life's intractable problems.

SUMMARY & ANALYSIS

Despite this dose of wary realism, Hosseini ends his often painful novel with hope. Flying the kite with Sohrab, Amir feels like a boy again, and for that time at least, he is innocent. It is also the first real connection he has with Sohrab since Sohrab stopped speaking. Flying the kite is his link to Sohrab much as it was once his link to Baba. The lifeless, vacant look leaves Sohrab's eyes as he gets ready to battle the other kite, and half a smile peeks out from his face, which is enough to mark the beginning of Sohrab's recovery in Amir's mind. A portent of what's to come, Sohrab's smile implies that the abuses of the past cannot dominate him or anyone forever, and that eventually Amir, Sohrab, and Afghanistan will look to the future and be healed. The novel comes full circle as it ends, with Amir going to run the kite for Sohrab. He says to Sohrab the last words Hassan said to him before Hassan was raped, but despite the fact that those were the circumstances the last time these words appeared in the book, the hopeful tone suggests Amir has paid his penance and found his redemption.

Important Quotations Explained

1. "That was a long time ago, but it's wrong what they say about the past, I've learned, about how you can bury it. Because the past claws its way out. Looking back now, I realize I have been peeking into that deserted alley for the last twenty-six years."

At the outset of chapter 1, just as the book begins, Amir writes these words. With them, he hints at the central drama of the story and the reason he is telling it. To the reader, the quotation functions as a teaser. It piques the reader's interest without revealing exactly what Amir is talking about, and from the timespan Amir mentions, twenty-six years, the reader gets an idea of just how important this moment was. As the story unfolds, we realize that the deserted alley Amir refers to is where Hassan was raped, and that this event has largely defined the course of Amir's life since. This is what Amir means when he says that the past continues to claw its way out. Try as he might to bury it, he was unable to because his feelings of guilt kept arising. As a result, he figuratively continues peeking into the alley where Assef raped Hassan, meaning that he keeps going over the event in his mind.

2. "A boy who won't stand up for himself becomes a man who can't stand up to anything."

Baba says these words to Rahim Khan while he is talking about Amir at the end of chapter 3, and the quotation reveals important traits in both Amir and Baba. With these words, Baba sums up one of Amir's major character flaws—his cowardice—and Baba shows how much value he places in standing up for what is right. Baba is reluctant to praise Amir, largely because he feels Amir lacks the courage to stand up for even himself, leaving Amir constantly craving Baba's approval. Amir's desire for this approval, as well as his cowardice later, cause him to let Assef rape Hassan. The quotation also foreshadows the major test of Amir's character that occurs when he must decide whether or not to return to Kabul to save Sohrab. As Amir searches for redemption, the question he struggles with is precisely what concerned Baba: does he have the courage and strength to stand up for what is right?

3.   "Huddled together in the dining room and waiting for the sun to rise, none of us had any notion that a way of life had ended." (p. 36)

This quotation occurs at the beginning of chapter 5, as Ali, Hassan, and Amir hide inside from the gunfire they hear in the street that signals the coup by Daoud Khan, which ended Afghanistan's monarchy. Though the effects of this coup were not immediately apparent, the coup ushered in an era of political instability that would essentially ruin Afghanistan. The way of life Amir refers to is the lifestyle that he, Baba, Ali, and Hassan knew before the coup, when Kabul was still safe and stable. For Amir in particular this meant a relatively idyllic life spent going to school, flying kites, and playing with Hassan, made possible because Baba was wealthy. But in the years after the night Amir describes when the coup occurred, violence and murder plagued the city, forcing Baba and Amir to leave Afghanistan and with it everything they owned. As a result, almost overnight everything Amir knew growing up in Kabul changed.

4.   "I actually *aspired* to cowardice, because the alternative, the real reason I was running, was that Assef was right: Nothing was free in this world. Maybe Hassan was the price I had to pay, the lamb I had to slay, to win Baba."

When Amir says this, toward the end of chapter 7, he has just watched Assef rape Hassan, and rather than intervene, he ran away. Amir says he aspired to cowardice because, in his estimation, what he did was worse than cowardice. If fear of being hurt by Assef were the main reason he ran, Amir suggests that at least it would have been more justified. Instead, he allowed the rape to happen because he wanted the blue kite, which he thought would prove to Baba that he was a winner like him, earning him Baba's love and approval. The price of the kite, as Amir says, was Hassan, and this is why Amir calls Hassan the lamb he had to slay. He draws a comparison between Hassan and the lamb sacrificed during the Muslim holiday of Eid Al-Adha to commemorate Abraham's near sacrifice of his son to God. In this context, Hassan was the sacrifice Amir had to make to get the kite and ultimately to gain Baba's affection.

5.   "My body was broken—just how badly I wouldn't find out until later—but I felt *healed*. Healed at last. I laughed."
     (p. 289)

This quotation occurs during Amir's meeting with Assef as he tries to find Sohrab in chapter 22. Assef beats Amir with brass knuckles, snapping Amir's ribs, splitting his lip and breaking both his jaw and the bone beneath his left eye, but because Amir feels he deserves this, he feels relief. He thinks he should have accepted the beating from Assef years ago, when he was given the choice of saving Hassan—and likely getting physically hurt—or letting Assef rape Hassan. Since that time, Amir has struggled with his guilt, which was only made worse by the fact that he was never punished for his actions. He had even gone looking for punishment in the past, as when he tried to get Hassan to hit him with the pomegranates, because he felt then there would at least be some justice for the way he treated Hassan. But Amir's guilt lingered until his confrontation with Assef, which despite the physical pain, made him feel psychologically healed. Thus, while Assef beat him, he began to laugh.

Key Facts

FULL TITLE
The Kite Runner

AUTHOR
Khaled Hosseini

TYPE OF WORK
Novel

GENRE
Bildungsroman; Redemption story

LANGUAGE
English

TIME AND PLACE WRITTEN
Los Angeles, CA; 2001–2003

DATE OF FIRST PUBLICATION
May 2003

PUBLISHER
Riverhead Books

NARRATOR
The Kite Runner is narrated by Amir four days after the final events of his decades-long story.

POINT OF VIEW
The narrator speaks in the first person, primarily describing events that occurred months and years ago. The narrator describes these events subjectively, explaining only how he experienced them. At one point, another character briefly narrates a chapter from his own point of view.

TONE
The tone is confessional, expressing profound remorse throughout the story

TENSE
Past tense with extended flashbacks

SETTING (TIME)
   1975 through 2001

SETTING (PLACE)
   Kabul, Afghanistan; California, United States

PROTAGONIST
   Amir

MAJOR CONFLICT
   After failing to intervene in the rape of his friend Hassan, Amir
   wrestles with his guilt and tries to find a way to atone for his
   actions.

RISING ACTION
   Forced out of Afghanistan by the Soviet invasion, Amir flees to
   the United States, where he tries to rebuild his life until an old
   friend offers him a way to make amends for his past.

CLIMAX
   Amir returns to Kabul, where he finds Hassan's son, Sohrab,
   and encounters Assef, the man who raped Hassan twenty-six
   years earlier.

FALLING ACTION
   Amir rescues Sohrab from a life of physical and sexual abuse
   and struggles to learn how he and Sohrab can recover from the
   traumas each has endured.

THEMES
   The search for redemption; the love and tension between
   fathers and sons; the intersection of political events and private
   lives; the persistence of the past

MOTIFS
   Rape; irony; regressing in time

SYMBOLS
   The cleft lip; kites; the lamb

FORESHADOWING
   Baba wonders if Amir will be able to stand up for what
   is right when the time comes; Baba worries that Islamic
   fundamentalists will one day control Afghanistan; Hassan
   threatens to shoot Assef's eye out; Assef vows revenge on Amir.

KEY FACTS

STUDY QUESTIONS AND ESSAY TOPICS

STUDY QUESTIONS

1. *What role does religion play in the lives of Baba, Amir, and Assef and in the novel as a whole?*

Though it is rarely the main focus, religion is nearly always present in Amir's narrative. It is part of the culture of Afghanistan, and it is, accordingly, a fixture of the everyday life Amir describes. Amir creates a complex portrait of both the positive and negative traits of religion, with the negative always stemming from fundamentalists who use their beliefs as an excuse to carry out violence against others and to limit people's freedoms. From what we learn of Baba's feelings toward religion, this is not surprising. The first significant episode in the book involving religion, for instance, occurs when Amir, who is still a child, tells Baba, as Baba pours a glass of whiskey, that the mullah at school called drinking alcohol a sin. Immediately, the scene establishes a contrast between Baba and the mullah. Baba calls the mullah and men like him bearded idiots and explains to Amir that theft, in its many variations, is the only true sin. Baba obviously does not respect the beliefs of the mullah, yet he still has his own moral code. Amir consequently grows up with a strong sense of morality, though it is entirely separate from Islam.

Yet religion also has a major role in determining the direction that Afghanistan takes in the years after Baba and Amir flee to the United States. Although Amir's narrative does not give a clear step-by-step account of the political events in Afghanistan, the reader does know that fighting continued in the country even after the departure of the Russians, called the Shorawi. Ultimately, the Taliban emerged with control, and from Amir's narrative we learn that many of the Afghans who left their country think the Islamist government the group has created is simply a means for them to justify their violence and authoritarian rule. The character who most represents this image of the Taliban is Assef, who tells Amir that he felt liberated while massacring Hazaras in their homes because he knew God was on his side. Ultimately, however, Assef's violence becomes his downfall when Sohrab shoots his eye out, and later, when Sohrab tries to kill himself, Amir has something of a religious conversion when Sohrab survives after Amir prays for God's help. Amir becomes an observant Muslim after that, but not a fundamentalist, making the case that religion is as good as the person practicing it.

2. *How does the author, Khaled Hosseini, use irony in the novel?*

Repeatedly throughout the book, Amir must face the unintended consequences of his actions. These situations are often ironic in that they are the exact opposite of what Amir intended, much as the man in Amir's first short story ends up unhappy because of his insatiable desire for wealth. In the most significant instances of irony, the irony stems from immorality. The most notable example of irony, for instance, centers on Amir's decision not to stop Assef from raping Hassan. Amir wanted to prove to Baba how much he was like him by bringing him the blue kite from the kite-fighting tournament, and he thought in doing so he would finally have the love that eluded him. While Amir gains more attention from Baba temporarily, he eventually loses Hassan, his best friend, because of his actions. A further irony becomes clear when Amir learns that Baba was actually Hassan's father. Baba had betrayed his own best friend, Ali, by conceiving Hassan with Ali's wife, and so Amir learns that he was, in fact, just like Baba in that sense, saddening Amir rather than making him happy.

3. *What is the significance of rape in the novel?*

Rape is among the most prominent motifs repeated in the novel. It is Hassan's rape that establishes the main drama of the story, and it is later Sohrab's rape by the Taliban that gives Amir the chance to redeem himself. The act of rape in this context carries a great deal of significance. First, it is presented as a form of perversion. What is typically considered an act shared by two people in love to conceive a child, as between Amir and Soraya, becomes an act of violence. Second, there is a distinct emotional component to rape. The rapist dominates the victim not only physically but psychologically as well, as we see in Hassan's rape and even more dramatically in Sohrab's. Finally, in each instance of rape we see, the rapist takes advantage of the social order, meaning the rapist is always in a position of greater power than the victim of the rape. Assef, for instance, is rich and has a politically powerful father, while Hassan is a poor Hazara. In each instance, rape acts as a symbolic violation of the powerless by those who have power.

SUGGESTED ESSAY TOPICS

1. *How do Amir and Hassan represent the divisions in Afghan society, and how do these divisions affect the course their lives take?*

2. *How does the author use time as a narrative device in the novel?*

3. *How do the political events that occur in Afghanistan shape the lives of Amir, Hassan, and Assef?*

4. *In what ways does Amir seek redemption, and why?*

5. *How do the relationships between fathers and sons affect the events of the novel?*

How to Write Literary Analysis

The Literary Essay: A Step-by-Step Guide

When you read for pleasure, your only goal is enjoyment. You might find yourself reading to get caught up in an exciting story, to learn about an interesting time or place, or just to pass time. Maybe you're looking for inspiration, guidance, or a reflection of your own life. There are as many different, valid ways of reading a book as there are books in the world.

When you read a work of literature in an English class, however, you're being asked to read in a special way: you're being asked to perform *literary analysis*. To analyze something means to break it down into smaller parts and then examine how those parts work, both individually and together. Literary analysis involves examining all the parts of a novel, play, short story, or poem—elements such as character, setting, tone, and imagery—and thinking about how the author uses those elements to create certain effects.

A literary essay isn't a book review: you're not being asked whether or not you liked a book or whether you'd recommend it to another reader. A literary essay also isn't like the kind of book report you wrote when you were younger, where your teacher wanted you to summarize the book's action. A high school- or college-level literary essay asks, "How does this piece of literature actually work?" "How does it do what it does?" and, "Why might the author have made the choices he or she did?"

The Seven Steps
No one is born knowing how to analyze literature; it's a skill you learn and a process you can master. As you gain more practice with this kind of thinking and writing, you'll be able to craft a method that works best for you. But until then, here are seven basic steps to writing a well-constructed literary essay:

1. Ask questions
2. Collect evidence
3. Construct a thesis

4. Develop and organize arguments
5. Write the introduction
6. Write the body paragraphs
7. Write the conclusion

---

1. ASK QUESTIONS

When you're assigned a literary essay in class, your teacher will often provide you with a list of writing prompts. Lucky you! Now all you have to do is choose one. Do yourself a favor and pick a topic that interests you. You'll have a much better (not to mention easier) time if you start off with something you enjoy thinking about. If you are asked to come up with a topic by yourself, though, you might start to feel a little panicked. Maybe you have too many ideas—or none at all. Don't worry. Take a deep breath and start by asking yourself these questions:

- **What struck you?** Did a particular image, line, or scene linger in your mind for a long time? If it fascinated you, chances are you can draw on it to write a fascinating essay.

- **What confused you?** Maybe you were surprised to see a character act in a certain way, or maybe you didn't understand why the book ended the way it did. Confusing moments in a work of literature are like a loose thread in a sweater: if you pull on it, you can unravel the entire thing. Ask yourself why the author chose to write about that character or scene the way he or she did and you might tap into some important insights about the work as a whole.

- **Did you notice any patterns?** Is there a phrase that the main character uses constantly or an image that repeats throughout the book? If you can figure out how that pattern weaves through the work and what the significance of that pattern is, you've almost got your entire essay mapped out.

- **Did you notice any contradictions or ironies?** Great works of literature are complex; great literary essays recognize and explain those complexities. Maybe the title (*Happy Days*) totally disagrees with the book's subject matter (hungry orphans dying in the woods). Maybe the main character acts one way around his family and a completely different way around his friends and associates. If you can find a way to explain a work's contradictory elements, you've got the seeds of a great essay.

At this point, you don't need to know exactly what you're going to say about your topic; you just need a place to begin your exploration. You can help direct your reading and brainstorming by formulating your topic as a *question,* which you'll then try to answer in your essay. The best questions invite critical debates and discussions, not just a rehashing of the summary. Remember, you're looking for something you can *prove or argue* based on evidence you find in the text. Finally, remember to keep the scope of your question in mind: is this a topic you can adequately address within the word or page limit you've been given? Conversely, is this a topic big enough to fill the required length?

GOOD QUESTIONS

"Are Romeo and Juliet's parents responsible for the deaths of their children?"

"Why do pigs keep showing up in LORD OF THE FLIES*?"*

"Are Dr. Frankenstein and his monster alike? How?"

BAD QUESTIONS

"What happens to Scout in TO KILL A MOCKINGBIRD*?"*

"What do the other characters in JULIUS CAESAR *think about Caesar?"*

"How does Hester Prynne in THE SCARLET LETTER *remind me of my sister?"*

---

2. COLLECT EVIDENCE

Once you know what question you want to answer, it's time to scour the book for things that will help you answer the question. Don't worry if you don't know what you want to say yet—right now you're just collecting ideas and material and letting it all percolate. Keep track of passages, symbols, images, or scenes that deal with your topic. Eventually, you'll start making connections between these examples and your thesis will emerge.

Here's a brief summary of the various parts that compose each and every work of literature. These are the elements that you will analyze in your essay, and which you will offer as evidence to support your arguments. For more on the parts of literary works, see the Glossary of Literary Terms at the end of this section.

ELEMENTS OF STORY   These are the *what*s of the work—what happens, where it happens, and to whom it happens.

- **Plot:** All of the events and actions of the work.
- **Character:** The people who act and are acted upon in a literary work. The main character of a work is known as the *protagonist*.
- **Conflict:** The central tension in the work. In most cases, the protagonist wants something, while opposing forces (antagonists) hinder the protagonist's progress.
- **Setting:** When and where the work takes place. Elements of setting include location, time period, time of day, weather, social atmosphere, and economic conditions.
- **Narrator:** The person telling the story. The narrator may straightforwardly report what happens, convey the subjective opinions and perceptions of one or more characters, or provide commentary and opinion in his or her own voice.
- **Themes:** The main idea or message of the work—usually an abstract idea about people, society, or life in general. A work may have many themes, which may be in tension with one another.

ELEMENTS OF STYLE   These are the *how*s—how the characters speak, how the story is constructed, and how language is used throughout the work.

- **Structure and organization:** How the parts of the work are assembled. Some novels are narrated in a linear, chronological fashion, while others skip around in time. Some plays follow a traditional three- or five-act structure, while others are a series of loosely connected scenes. Some authors deliberately leave gaps in their works, leaving readers to puzzle out the missing information. A work's structure and organization can tell you a lot about the kind of message it wants to convey.
- **Point of view:** The perspective from which a story is told. In *first-person point of view*, the narrator involves him or herself in the story. ("I went to the store"; "We watched in horror as the bird slammed into the window.") A first-person narrator is usually the protagonist of the work, but not always. In *third-person point of view*, the narrator does not participate

in the story. A third-person narrator may closely follow a specific character, recounting that individual character's thoughts or experiences, or it may be what we call an *omniscient* narrator. Omniscient narrators see and know all: they can witness any event in any time or place and are privy to the inner thoughts and feelings of all characters. Remember that the narrator and the author are not the same thing!

- **Diction:** Word choice. Whether a character uses dry, clinical language or flowery prose with lots of exclamation points can tell you a lot about his or her attitude and personality.

- **Syntax:** Word order and sentence construction. Syntax is a crucial part of establishing an author's narrative voice. Ernest Hemingway, for example, is known for writing in very short, straightforward sentences, while James Joyce characteristically wrote in long, incredibly complicated lines.

- **Tone:** The mood or feeling of the text. Diction and syntax often contribute to the tone of a work. A novel written in short, clipped sentences that use small, simple words might feel brusque, cold, or matter-of-fact.

- **Imagery:** Language that appeals to the senses, representing things that can be seen, smelled, heard, tasted, or touched.

- **Figurative language:** Language that is not meant to be interpreted literally. The most common types of figurative language are *metaphors* and *similes,* which compare two unlike things in order to suggest a similarity between them— for example, "All the world's a stage," or "The moon is like a ball of green cheese." (Metaphors say one thing *is* another thing; similes claim that one thing is *like* another thing.)

3. CONSTRUCT A THESIS

When you've examined all the evidence you've collected and know how you want to answer the question, it's time to write your thesis statement. A *thesis* is a claim about a work of literature that needs to be supported by evidence and arguments. The thesis statement is the heart of the literary essay, and the bulk of your paper will be spent trying to prove this claim. A good thesis will be:

- **Arguable.** "*The Great Gatsby* describes New York society in the 1920s" isn't a thesis—it's a fact.

- **Provable through textual evidence.** "*Hamlet* is a confusing but ultimately very well-written play" is a weak thesis because it offers the writer's personal opinion about the book. Yes, it's arguable, but it's not a claim that can be proved or supported with examples taken from the play itself.

- **Surprising.** "Both George and Lenny change a great deal in *Of Mice and Men*" is a weak thesis because it's obvious. A really strong thesis will argue for a reading of the text that is not immediately apparent.

- **Specific.** "Dr. Frankenstein's monster tells us a lot about the human condition" is *almost* a really great thesis statement, but it's still too vague. What does the writer mean by "a lot"? *How* does the monster tell us so much about the human condition?

GOOD THESIS STATEMENTS

Question: In *Romeo and Juliet*, which is more powerful in shaping the lovers' story: fate or foolishness?

Thesis: "Though Shakespeare defines Romeo and Juliet as 'star-crossed lovers' and images of stars and planets appear throughout the play, a closer examination of that celestial imagery reveals that the stars are merely witnesses to the characters' foolish activities and not the causes themselves."

Question: How does the bell jar function as a symbol in Sylvia Plath's *The Bell Jar*?

Thesis: "A bell jar is a bell-shaped glass that has three basic uses: to hold a specimen for observation, to contain gases, and to maintain a vacuum. The bell jar appears in each of these capacities in *The Bell Jar*, Plath's semi-autobiographical novel, and each appearance marks a different stage in Esther's mental breakdown."

Question: Would Piggy in *The Lord of the Flies* make a good island leader if he were given the chance?

Thesis: "Though the intelligent, rational, and innovative Piggy has the mental characteristics of a good leader, he ultimately lacks the social skills necessary to be an effective one. Golding emphasizes this point by giving Piggy a foil in the charismatic Jack, whose magnetic personality allows him to capture and wield power effectively, if not always wisely."

LITERARY ANALYSIS

4. Develop and Organize Arguments

The reasons and examples that support your thesis will form the middle paragraphs of your essay. Since you can't really write your thesis statement until you know how you'll structure your argument, you'll probably end up working on steps 3 and 4 at the same time.

There's no single method of argumentation that will work in every context. One essay prompt might ask you to compare and contrast two characters, while another asks you to trace an image through a given work of literature. These questions require different kinds of answers and therefore different kinds of arguments. Below, we'll discuss three common kinds of essay prompts and some strategies for constructing a solid, well-argued case.

Types of Literary Essays

- **Compare and contrast**

    Compare and contrast the characters of Huck and Jim in The Adventures of Huckleberry Finn.

    Chances are you've written this kind of essay before. In an academic literary context, you'll organize your arguments the same way you would in any other class. You can either go *subject by subject* or *point by point*. In the former, you'll discuss one character first and then the second. In the latter, you'll choose several traits (attitude toward life, social status, images and metaphors associated with the character) and devote a paragraph to each. You may want to use a mix of these two approaches—for example, you may want to spend a paragraph apiece broadly sketching Huck's and Jim's personalities before transitioning into a paragraph or two that describes a few key points of comparison. This can be a highly effective strategy if you want to make a counterintuitive argument—that, despite seeming to be totally different, the two objects being compared are actually similar in a very important way (or vice versa). Remember that your essay should reveal something fresh or unexpected about the text, so think beyond the obvious parallels and differences.

- **Trace**

    Choose an image—for example, birds, knives, or eyes—and trace that image throughout Macbeth.

    Sounds pretty easy, right? All you need to do is read the play, underline every appearance of a knife in *Macbeth,* and then list them in your essay in the order they appear, right? Well, not exactly. Your teacher doesn't want a simple catalog of examples. He or she wants to see you make *connections* between those examples—that's the difference between summarizing and analyzing. In the *Macbeth* example above, think about the different contexts in which knives appear in the play and to what effect. In *Macbeth,* there are real knives and imagined knives; knives that kill and knives that simply threaten. Categorize and classify your examples to give them some order. Finally, always keep the overall effect in mind. After you choose and analyze your examples, you should come to some greater understanding about the work, as well as your chosen image, symbol, or phrase's role in developing the major themes and stylistic strategies of that work.

- **Debate**

  Is the society depicted in 1984 *good for its citizens?*

  In this kind of essay, you're being asked to debate a moral, ethical, or aesthetic issue regarding the work. You might be asked to judge a character or group of characters (*Is Caesar responsible for his own demise?*) or the work itself (*Is* JANE EYRE *a feminist novel?*). For this kind of essay, there are two important points to keep in mind. First, don't simply base your arguments on your personal feelings and reactions. Every literary essay expects you to read and analyze the work, so search for evidence in the text. What do characters in *1984* have to say about the government of Oceania? What images does Orwell use that might give you a hint about his attitude toward the government? As in any debate, you also need to make sure that you define all the necessary terms before you begin to argue your case. What does it mean to be a "good" society? What makes a novel "feminist"? You should define your terms right up front, in the first paragraph after your introduction.

  Second, remember that strong literary essays make contrary and surprising arguments. Try to think outside the box. In the *1984* example above, it seems like the obvious answer would be no, the totalitarian society depicted in Orwell's novel is *not* good for its citizens. But can you think of any arguments for the opposite side? Even if your final assertion is that the novel depicts a cruel, repressive, and therefore harmful society, acknowledging and responding to the counterargument will strengthen your overall case.

5. WRITE THE INTRODUCTION

Your introduction sets up the entire essay. It's where you present your topic and articulate the particular issues and questions you'll be addressing. It's also where you, as the writer, introduce yourself to your readers. A persuasive literary essay immediately establishes its writer as a knowledgeable, authoritative figure.

An introduction can vary in length depending on the overall length of the essay, but in a traditional five-paragraph essay it should be no longer than one paragraph. However long it is, your introduction needs to:

- **Provide any necessary context.** Your introduction should situate the reader and let him or her know what to expect. What book are you discussing? Which characters? What topic will you be addressing?

- **Answer the "So what?" question.** Why is this topic important, and why is your particular position on the topic noteworthy? Ideally, your introduction should pique the reader's interest by suggesting how your argument is surprising or otherwise counterintuitive. Literary essays make unexpected connections and reveal less-than-obvious truths.

- **Present your thesis.** This usually happens at or very near the end of your introduction.

- **Indicate the shape of the essay to come.** Your reader should finish reading your introduction with a good sense of the scope of your essay as well as the path you'll take toward proving your thesis. You don't need to spell out every step, but you do need to suggest the organizational pattern you'll be using.

Your introduction should not:

- **Be vague.** Beware of the two killer words in literary analysis: *interesting* and *important*. Of course the work, question, or example is interesting and important—that's why you're writing about it!

- **Open with any grandiose assertions.** Many student readers think that beginning their essays with a flamboyant statement such as, "Since the dawn of time, writers have been fascinated with the topic of free will," makes them sound important and commanding. You know what? It actually sounds pretty amateurish.

- **Wildly praise the work.** Another typical mistake student writers make is extolling the work or author. Your teacher doesn't need to be told that "Shakespeare is perhaps the greatest writer in the English language." You can mention a work's reputation in passing—by referring to *The Adventures of Huckleberry Finn* as "Mark Twain's enduring classic," for example—but don't make a point of bringing it up unless that reputation is key to your argument.

- **Go off-topic.** Keep your introduction streamlined and to the point. Don't feel the need to throw in all kinds of bells and whistles in order to impress your reader—just get to the point as quickly as you can, without skimping on any of the required steps.

---

6. WRITE THE BODY PARAGRAPHS

Once you've written your introduction, you'll take the arguments you developed in step 4 and turn them into your body paragraphs. The organization of this middle section of your essay will largely be determined by the argumentative strategy you use, but no matter how you arrange your thoughts, your body paragraphs need to do the following:

- **Begin with a strong topic sentence.** Topic sentences are like signs on a highway: they tell the reader where they are and where they're going. A good topic sentence not only alerts readers to what issue will be discussed in the following paragraph but also gives them a sense of what argument will be made *about* that issue. "Rumor and gossip play an important role in *The Crucible*" isn't a strong topic sentence because it doesn't tell us very much. "The community's constant gossiping creates an environment that allows false accusations to flourish" is a much stronger topic sentence— it not only tells us *what* the paragraph will discuss (gossip) but *how* the paragraph will discuss the topic (by showing how gossip creates a set of conditions that leads to the play's climactic action).

- **Fully and completely develop a single thought.** Don't skip around in your paragraph or try to stuff in too much material. Body paragraphs are like bricks: each individual one needs to be strong and sturdy or the entire structure will collapse. Make sure you have really proven your point before moving on to the next one.

- **Use transitions effectively.** Good literary essay writers know that each paragraph must be clearly and strongly linked to the material around it. Think of each paragraph as a response to the one that precedes it. Use transition words and phrases such as *however, similarly, on the contrary, therefore,* and *furthermore* to indicate what kind of response you're making.

---

7. WRITE THE CONCLUSION

Just as you used the introduction to ground your readers in the topic before providing your thesis, you'll use the conclusion to quickly summarize the specifics learned thus far and then hint at the broader implications of your topic. A good conclusion will:

- **Do more than simply restate the thesis.** If your thesis argued that *The Catcher in the Rye* can be read as a Christian allegory, don't simply end your essay by saying, "And that is why *The Catcher in the Rye* can be read as a Christian allegory." If you've constructed your arguments well, this kind of statement will just be redundant.

- **Synthesize the arguments, not summarize them.** Similarly, don't repeat the details of your body paragraphs in your conclusion. The reader has already read your essay, and chances are it's not so long that they've forgotten all your points by now.

- **Revisit the "So what?" question.** In your introduction, you made a case for why your topic and position are important. You should close your essay with the same sort of gesture. What do your readers know now that they didn't know before? How will that knowledge help them better appreciate or understand the work overall?

- **Move from the specific to the general.** Your essay has most likely treated a very specific element of the work—a single character, a small set of images, or a particular passage. In your conclusion, try to show how this narrow discussion has wider implications for the work overall. If your essay on *To Kill a Mockingbird* focused on the character of Boo Radley, for example, you might want to include a bit in your conclusion about how he fits into the novel's larger message about childhood, innocence, or family life.

- **Stay relevant.** Your conclusion should suggest new directions of thought, but it shouldn't be treated as an opportunity to pad your essay with all the extra, interesting ideas you came up with during your brainstorming sessions but couldn't fit into the essay proper. Don't attempt to stuff in unrelated queries or too many abstract thoughts.

- **Avoid making overblown closing statements.** A conclusion should open up your highly specific, focused discussion, but it should do so without drawing a sweeping lesson about life or human nature. Making such observations may be part of the point of reading, but it's almost always a mistake in essays, where these observations tend to sound overly dramatic or simply silly.

A+ Essay Checklist

Congratulations! If you've followed all the steps we've outlined above, you should have a solid literary essay to show for all your efforts. What if you've got your sights set on an A+? To write the kind of superlative essay that will be rewarded with a perfect grade, keep the following rubric in mind. These are the qualities that teachers expect to see in a truly A+ essay. How does yours stack up?

- ✓ Demonstrates a thorough understanding of the book
- ✓ Presents an original, compelling argument
- ✓ Thoughtfully analyzes the text's formal elements
- ✓ Uses appropriate and insightful examples
- ✓ Structures ideas in a logical and progressive order
- ✓ Demonstrates a mastery of sentence construction, transitions, grammar, spelling, and word choice

LITERARY ANALYSIS

A+ Student Essay

> What examples of sexual victimization take place in the
> novel? What do they suggest about Afghanistan?

Whatever form victimization takes, political, social, economic, or any
other kind, it's about the powerful taking advantage of the powerless. Several examples of this dynamic appear throughout *The Kite
Runner*, but the most graphic by far are the instances of sexual victimization. They occur at intervals throughout Amir's story, and in each
instance they reflect the imbalance of power in Afghan society.

The most significant and symbolic example of this is Hassan's
rape. Although it's a sexual act, the point isn't sexual gratification.
Assef wants to show his dominance over Hassan. Hassan is a Hazara,
an ethnic minority in Afghanistan. The act is intended to show Hassan
that, as a Hazara, he is basically powerless. In that way it reinforces
the social structure we see more broadly in Kabul. The Hazaras are
socially stigmatized, which in turn means they generally have to
work menial jobs and tend to be poor. In other words, they have less
social, political, and financial power than their counterparts. Assef,
being from a rich and well-connected Pashtun family, is the exact
opposite of a Hazara in this regard. His rape of Hassan symbolically
demonstrates this imbalance of power.

A later act of sexual victimization, though the purpose is
ultimately sexual gratification, is also about power. As Amir and
Baba flee Afghanistan after the Soviet invasion, the truck they're in
is stopped at a checkpoint, and one of the Russian guards demands
half an hour with one of the female refugees before they can pass.
The attempted rape is stopped, but it still reveals a great deal about
who holds power. With their invasion, the Soviets essentially took
Afghanistan hostage. The balance of power in the country shifted
drastically, with even those in the ruling class losing a great deal as
Russian guns and tanks rolled in. This shift plays out symbolically
with the Russian guard demanding sex from the female refugee.
He is in a position of power over the men and women in the truck
since he controls whether they're allowed through to Pakistan, and
he tries to use that power to his advantage. The woman and the
others with her are helpless to do anything about it. Although Baba
intervenes, he's almost killed for it. It's another Russian who actually
stops the rape.

Toward the end of the novel there is a final act of sexual victimization, again involving Assef. This time, however, the power dynamic in play is slightly different. Amir discovers that Assef is holding Hassan's son, Sohrab, and it appears from the situation and the way the boy is dressed that he's being kept as a sex slave. What's changed since Assef raped Hassan is that he is now a member of the Taliban, which now rules Afghanistan, having taken back control of the country from the Soviets. Although there's still an undercurrent of Pashtun dominance of the Hazaras in this situation, since Sohrab is a Hazara, as was his father, the main power relationship involved is that of the Taliban versus the rest of Afghanistan. It's Assef's status as a member of the Taliban that confers on him his power, and thus his ability to sexually abuse Sohrab with impunity.

Each instance of rape is representative of one of the major struggles in Afghanistan's recent history. First is the longstanding ethnic tension between the Pashtuns and Hazaras, later comes the Soviet invasion, and then the Taliban comes into power. The suggestion made by the novel is that in every one of these instances Afghanistan itself has been victimized and damaged by the resulting imbalance of power, as well as by the willingness of those in authority to prey upon and abuse the weakest, most vulnerable segments of its own population.

Glossary of Literary Terms

ANTAGONIST

The entity that acts to frustrate the goals of the *protagonist*. The antagonist is usually another *character* but may also be a non-human force.

ANTIHERO / ANTIHEROINE

A *protagonist* who is not admirable or who challenges notions of what should be considered admirable.

CHARACTER

A person, animal, or any other thing with a personality that appears in a *narrative*.

CLIMAX

The moment of greatest intensity in a text or the major turning point in the *plot*.

CONFLICT

The central struggle that moves the *plot* forward. The conflict can be the *protagonist*'s struggle against fate, nature, society, or another person.

FIRST-PERSON POINT OF VIEW

A literary style in which the *narrator* tells the story from his or her own *point of view* and refers to himself or herself as "I." The narrator may be an active participant in the story or just an observer.

HERO / HEROINE

The principal *character* in a literary work or *narrative*.

IMAGERY

Language that brings to mind sense-impressions, representing things that can be seen, smelled, heard, tasted, or touched.

MOTIF

A recurring idea, structure, contrast, or device that develops or informs the major *themes* of a work of literature.

NARRATIVE

A story.

NARRATOR

The person (sometimes a *character*) who tells a story; the *voice* assumed by the writer. The narrator and the author of the work of literature are not the same person.

PLOT

The arrangement of the events in a story, including the sequence in which they are told, the relative emphasis they are given, and the causal connections between events.

POINT OF VIEW

The *perspective* that a *narrative* takes toward the events it describes.

PROTAGONIST

The main *character* around whom the story revolves.

SETTING

The location of a *narrative* in time and space. Setting creates mood or atmosphere.

SUBPLOT

A secondary *plot* that is of less importance to the overall story but may serve as a point of contrast or comparison to the main plot.

SYMBOL

An object, *character,* figure, or color that is used to represent an abstract idea or concept. Unlike an *emblem,* a symbol may have different meanings in different contexts.

SYNTAX

The way the words in a piece of writing are put together to form lines, phrases, or clauses; the basic structure of a piece of writing.

THEME

A fundamental and universal idea explored in a literary work.

TONE

The author's attitude toward the subject or *characters* of a story or poem or toward the reader.

VOICE

An author's individual way of using language to reflect his or her own personality and attitudes. An author communicates voice through *tone, diction,* and *syntax.*

LITERARY ANALYSIS

A Note on Plagiarism

Plagiarism—presenting someone else's work as your own—rears its ugly head in many forms. Many students know that copying text without citing it is unacceptable. But some don't realize that even if you're not quoting directly, but instead are paraphrasing or summarizing, *it is plagiarism* unless you cite the source.

Here are the most common forms of plagiarism:

- Using an author's phrases, sentences, or paragraphs without citing the source
- Paraphrasing an author's ideas without citing the source
- Passing off another student's work as your own

How do you steer clear of plagiarism? You should *always* acknowledge all words and ideas that aren't your own by using quotation marks around verbatim text or citations like footnotes and endnotes to note another writer's ideas. For more information on how to give credit when credit is due, ask your teacher for guidance or visit www.sparknotes.com.

REVIEW AND RESOURCES

QUIZ

1. What is a kite runner?

   A. Someone who competes in the kite-fighting tournament
   B. Someone who makes and sells kites
   C. Someone who retrieves the losing kite in a kite battle
   D. Someone who is exceptionally skilled at flying kites

2. How did Ali come into Baba's family?

   A. Ali's parents were killed, and Baba's father, who judged the murder trial, took him in
   B. He was born to the Hazara servant of Baba's father
   C. He killed a sheep belonging to Baba's family and was forced to become their servant as punishment
   D. Baba and Ali had the same father

3. What is it that worries Baba about Amir?

   A. He isn't certain who Amir's mother was
   B. A boy who can't stand up for himself becomes a man who can't stand up to anything
   C. Boys at school bully Amir
   D. Amir could disappoint him by losing the kite-fighting tournament

4. How is Hassan's cleft lip fixed?

   A. Amir uses his birthday money to pay for the surgery
   B. Baba pays for the surgery as a birthday gift to Hassan
   C. Hassan steals Amir's birthday money and uses it for the surgery
   D. Ali steals Amir's birthday money to pay for the surgery

5. Why does Amir think Baba doesn't love him fully?

   A. Baba holds him responsible for the death of his wife (Amir's mother), who died giving birth to Amir
   B. Because Amir never did well in the kite-fighting tournament
   C. Baba questions whether Amir is his biological son
   D. Baba prefers to fly kites with Hassan

6. Why doesn't Amir stop Hassan's rape?

   A. He believes Hassan, who is a Hazara, deserves to learn a lesson
   B. He thinks Hassan wouldn't have helped him if the roles were reversed
   C. He and Hassan make eye contact and Hassan silently tells Amir to run
   D. He is afraid and also wants the blue kite, which he can only get by not interfering

7. What does Amir put under Hassan's mattress to frame him?

   A. His favorite book and the watch Baba gave him
   B. The kite Baba bought him that he used to win the kite-fighting tournament
   C. Money he received for his birthday and the watch Baba gave him
   D. A ski mask, a length of rope, and a handful of gold coins

8. Why do Baba and Amir leave Kabul?

   A. One of Baba's old enemies has found Baba and wants to take revenge
   B. The new president created a totalitarian dictatorship when he took power
   C. The Taliban threaten to kill Baba
   D. The invasion by the Russians has turned the country into a dangerous war zone

9.   When Baba and Amir flee Kabul, what does Baba say to the Russian guard who tries to rape the woman in the truck with them?

    A.   He tells the guard that rape is a sin against God

    B.   He calls the guard a coward who couldn't get a woman without a gun

    C.   He says decency is even more important in times of war

    D.   He threatens to kill the guard if the guard touches the woman

10.   Where do Baba and Amir end up in the U.S.?

    A.   Los Angeles, California

    B.   Newark, New Jersey

    C.   Reno, Nevada

    D.   Fremont, California

11.   What does Amir decide to study in college?

    A.   English

    B.   Farsi literature

    C.   Medicine

    D.   Law

12.   Where does Amir meet Soraya?

    A.   The local mosque

    B.   A gathering of Afghans in the park

    C.   At school

    D.   The flea market

13. When Baba is diagnosed with lung cancer and Amir says he doesn't know what to do without him, what does Baba tell Amir?

   A. Amir needs to quit crying and accept that he will be alone soon
   B. That he has been trying to teach Amir how to live without him for Amir's whole life
   C. Amir needs to have faith that God will provide for him
   D. That Amir should find Hassan to make up for the ways he wronged him

14. Which accurately describes the traditional Afghan way of proposing marriage, which we see in the novel?

   A. The man proposes to the woman in front of her family
   B. The man asks for consent from the woman's father
   C. The man's father asks consent from the woman's father
   D. The man tells the woman's mother his intentions, then proposes to the woman

15. What do Amir and Soraya want to do but are not able to?

   A. Move back to Kabul
   B. Buy a house
   C. Leave Afghanistan behind and live as Americans
   D. Have a baby

16. What does Rahim Khan say to Amir to convince Amir to go to Pakistan?

   A. There is a way to be good again
   B. The past is gone and buried
   C. Hassan wants to see you
   D. I have money that is yours

17. Who is Hassan's real father?

   A. Rahim Khan
   B. Ali
   C. Baba
   D. General Taheri

REVIEW & RESOURCES

18.   Why does Rahim Khan want Amir to go to Kabul?

   A.   So he can check on Baba's house, which has been
        claimed by the Taliban
   B.   So he can confront Assef about his rape of Hassan
   C.   So he can get Sohrab and bring him back to Pakistan
   D.   So he can find Hassan

19.   Why does Farid initially dislike Amir?

   A.   Amir was condescending towards him
   B.   Rahim Khan told Farid what Amir had done to Hassan
   C.   Amir is Sunni, while Farid is Shia
   D.   Farid thought Amir was returning to Kabul to sell
        property

20.   What do Farid and Amir see during the half-time show of the
      soccer game in Kabul?

   A.   A man and a woman stoned to death
   B.   A thief who has his hand cut off
   C.   A display of horseback riding by members of the
        Taliban
   D.   A wedding ceremony

21.   Why does Amir laugh when Assef beats him?

   A.   He has gone crazy
   B.   He has been drugged
   C.   He feels relief from his guilt
   D.   He feels Assef can't hurt him

22.   Why is it significant that Sohrab shoots out Assef's eye with
      his slingshot?

   A.   Amir and Hassan used to hunt birds with a slingshot
        as children
   B.   Hassan once saved Amir from Assef with a slingshot
   C.   Assef used to threaten Amir and Hassan with a
        slingshot
   D.   Amir taught Hassan how to shoot a slingshot when
        they were children

23. Why does Amir have difficulty adopting Sohrab?

   A.   Amir is no longer a citizen of Afghanistan
   B.   Amir has no papers proving Sohrab's parents are dead
   C.   Amir refuses to pay the bribe demanded by the
        adoption officials
   D.   Amir is considered a traitor for having fled
        Afghanistan

24. What will Sohrab no longer do after he attempts suicide?

   A.   Speak
   B.   Use his slingshot
   C.   Fly his kite
   D.   Pray

25. What metaphor does Amir use to explain the importance of
     Sohrab smiling?

   A.   The longest journeys begin with a single step
   B.   When spring comes, it melts the snow one flake at a
        time
   C.   The storm is most dangerous just before it clears
   D.   Every wound has its purpose

ANSWER KEY

1: C; 2: A; 3: B; 4: B; 5: A; 6: D; 7: C; 8: D; 9: C; 10: D; 11: A; 12: D; 13: B; 14: C; 15: D; 16: A; 17: C; 18: C; 19: D; 20: A; 21: C; 22: B; 23: B; 24: A; 25: B.

Suggestions for Further Reading

Bloom, Harold, ed. *Bloom's Guides: Khaled Hosseini's* The Kite Runner. New York: Chelsea House Publishers, 2009.

Ewans, Martin. *Afghanistan: A Short History of Its People and Politics.* New York: Harper Perennial, 2002.

Grossman, Lev. "The Kite Runner Author Returns Home." *Time,* May 17, 2007.

Hayes, Judi Slayden. *In Search of* The Kite Runner. Atlanta: Chalice Press, 2007.

Herbert, Marilyn. *Bookclub-In-A-Box: Discusses the Novel The Kite Runner by Khaled Hosseini.* Toronto: Bookclub-In-A-Box, 2006.

O'Rourke, Meghan. "*The Kite Runner:* Do I really have to read it?" *Slate,* July 25, 2005.

Sherman, Sue. *Cambridge Wizard Student Guide: The Kite Runner.* New York: Cambridge University Press, 2006.

SPARKNOTES LITERATURE GUIDES

1984

The Adventures of Huckleberry Finn

The Adventures of Tom Sawyer

The Alchemist

The Aeneid

All Quiet on the Western Front

And Then There Were None

Angela's Ashes

Animal Farm

Anna Karenina

Anne of Green Gables

Anthem

Antony and Cleopatra

Aristotle's Ethics

As I Lay Dying

As You Like It

Atlas Shrugged

The Autobiography of Malcolm X

The Awakening

The Bean Trees

The Bell Jar

Beloved

Beowulf

Billy Budd

Black Boy

Bless Me, Ultima

The Bluest Eye

Brave New World

The Brothers Karamazov

The Call of the Wild

Candide

The Canterbury Tales

Catch-22

The Catcher in the Rye

The Chocolate War

The Chosen

Cold Mountain

Cold Sassy Tree

The Color Purple

The Count of Monte Cristo

Crime and Punishment

The Crucible

Cry, the Beloved Country

The Curious Incident of the Dog in the Night-Time

Cyrano de Bergerac

David Copperfield

Death of a Salesman

The Death of Socrates

The Diary of a Young Girl

A Doll's House

Don Quixote

Dr. Faustus

Dr. Jekyll and Mr. Hyde

Dracula

Dune

Mythology

Emma

Ethan Frome

Fahrenheit 451

Fallen Angels

A Farewell to Arms

Farewell to Manzanar

Flowers for Algernon

For Whom the Bell Tolls

The Fountainhead

Frankenstein

The Giver

The Glass Menagerie

Gone With the Wind

The Good Earth

The Grapes of Wrath

Great Expectations

The Great Gatsby

Grendel

Gulliver's Travels

Hamlet

The Handmaid's Tale

Hard Times

Harry Potter and the Sorcerer's Stone

Heart of Darkness

Henry IV, Part I

Henry V

Hiroshima

The Hobbit

The House of Seven Gables

The Hunger Games

I Know Why the Caged Bird Sings

The Iliad

Inferno

Inherit the Wind

Invisible Man

Jane Eyre

Johnny Tremain

The Joy Luck Club

Julius Caesar

The Jungle

The Killer Angels

The Kite Runner

King Lear

The Last of the Mohicans

Les Misérables

A Lesson Before Dying

The Little Prince

Little Women

Lord of the Flies

The Lord of the Rings

Macbeth

Madame Bovary

A Man for All Seasons

The Mayor of Casterbridge

The Merchant of Venice

A Midsummer Night's Dream

Moby-Dick

Much Ado About Nothing

My Antonia

Narrative of the Life of Frederick Douglass

Native Son

The New Testament

Night

Notes from Underground

The Odyssey

The Oedipus Plays

Of Mice and Men

The Old Man and the Sea

The Old Testament

Oliver Twist

The Once and Future King

One Day in the Life of Ivan Denisovich

One Flew Over the Cuckoo's Nest

One Hundred Years of Solitude

Othello

Our Town

The Outsiders

Paradise Lost

A Passage to India

The Pearl

The Picture of Dorian Gray

Poe's Short Stories

A Portrait of the Artist as a Young Man

Pride and Prejudice

The Prince

A Raisin in the Sun

The Red Badge of Courage

The Republic

Richard III

Robinson Crusoe

Romeo and Juliet

The Scarlet Letter

A Separate Peace

Silas Marner

Sir Gawain and the Green Knight

Slaughterhouse-Five

Snow Falling on Cedars

Song of Solomon

The Sound and the Fury

Steppenwolf

The Stranger

A Streetcar Named Desire

The Sun Also Rises

A Tale of Two Cities

The Taming of the Shrew

The Tempest

Tess of the d'Urbervilles

The Things They Carried

Their Eyes Were Watching God

Things Fall Apart

To Kill a Mockingbird

To the Lighthouse

Treasure Island

Twelfth Night

Ulysses

Uncle Tom's Cabin

Walden

War and Peace

Wuthering Heights

A Yellow Raft in Blue Water